Y0-DWW-044

Berg Women's Series

General Editor: MIRIAM KOCHAN

Gertrude Bell   SUSAN GOODMAN
Mme de Staël   RENEE WINEGARTEN
Emily Dickinson DONNA DICKENSON

Emily Dickinson

Donna Dickenson

BERG *Leamington Spa/Dover NH/Heidelberg*

© copyright Berg Publishers 1985

British Library Cataloguing in Publication Data

Dickenson, Donna
  Emily Dickinson.—(Berg women's series)
  1. Dickinson, Emily—Biography   2. Poets,
  American—19th century—Biography
  I. Title
  811'.4   PS1541.Z/

ISBN 0 907582 88 5
    0 907582 69 9 (pbk)

Library of Congress Cataloging-in-Publication Data

Dickenson, Donna
  Emily Dickinson.

  (Berg women's series)
  Bibliography: p.
  1. Dickinson, Emily, 1830 – 1886—Biography. 2. Poets,
American—19th century—Biography.   I. Title.
II. Series.
PS1541.Z5D48   1985   811'.4   85 – 13057
ISBN 0 – 907582 – 69 – 9 (pbk.)
ISBN 0 – 907582 – 88 – 5

All rights reserved. No part of this publication
may be reproduced, stored in a retrieval system, or
transmitted in any form or by any means, electronic,
mechanical, photocopying or otherwise, without the
prior permission of Berg Publishers Ltd.

Published in 1985 by **Berg Publishers Ltd**,
24 Binswood Avenue, Leamington Spa, CV32 5SQ, UK
51 Washington Street,
Dover, New Hampshire 03820, USA
Panoramastr. 118,
6900 Heidelberg, West Germany

Contents

Illustrations

Acknowledgments

Grateful acknowledgment is made to Harvard University Press for their permission to reproduce poems or sections of poems from Thomas H. Johnson's definitive variorum edition of Dickinson's poems. I have followed Johnson's numbering throughout.

Much of the material in the chronology is abridged from Richard Sewall's *Life of Emily Dickinson* (1974).

'New England', by Edwin Arlington Robinson: reprinted with permission of Macmillan Publishing Company from *Collected Poems*, Edwin Arlington Robinson. Copyright 1925 by Edwin Arlington Robinson, renewed 1953 by Ruth Nivison and Barbara R. Holt.

'Provide, Provide', by Robert Frost: from *The Poetry of Robert Frost*, edited by Edward Connery Latham. Copyright © 1969 by Holt, Rinehart and Winston. © 1964 by Lesley Frost Ballentine. Reprinted by kind permission of Holt, Rinehart and Winston, Publishers, and of Jonathan Cape Ltd.

TV poem by Adrienne Rich on p. 68, referred to hirl. 'E' (see note 1, p. 83), is 'I am in danger — Sir —': Reprinted from *Poems Selected and New 1950 to 1974*, by Adrienne Rich, by permission of W. W. Norton & Co. Inc. Copyright © 1975, 1973, 1971, 1969, 1966 by W. W. Norton & Co. Inc.

Every effort has been made to trace all copyright holders, but if any have been inadvertently overlooked the publisher will be pleased to make the necessary arrangements at the first opportunity.

To Chris

Love – is anterior to Life –
Posterior – to Death –
Initial of Creation, and
The Exponent of Earth –   (917, c. 1864)

I have no portrait, now, but am small, like the Wren, and my Hair is bold, like the Chestnut Burr – and my eyes, like the Sherry in the Glass, that the Guest leaves . . . It often alarms Father – He says Death might occur, and he has molds of all the rest – but has no Mold of me, but I noticed the Quick wore off these things, in a few days, and forestall the dishonor –

— *Letter to Thomas Wentworth Higginson, July 1862*

Introduction

In her lifetime Emily Dickinson saw her name in print only once
— when she won second prize for rye and Indian bread at the
Amherst show. Since her death, and particularly in the thirty
years since the definitive edition of her poems, her name has
become familiar to the point of surfeit. Is there any call for yet
another book about Emily Dickinson? What can this book offer
that other authors have not covered?

There is a need for a short book which straddles the gap
between detailed scholarly criticism of Dickinson and the out-
dated popular image of the lovelorn recluse. I have tried to
present the right sort of material to do this: a wide range of both
early and late poems, enough detail about Dickinson's life and
background to illuminate but not dazzle the reader, and an
examination of the radical change in critical opinion. Throughout
the book I have striven to put the poems first, to explain the life
through them as an important but secondary concern. This is
really all we can do: Dickinson left few letters and little biographical material. Yet the great tendency has been to concentrate on
the life instead, to construct myths where detail is wanting — and
it is almost always wanting.

There is an enormous amount of writing about Dickinson, but
she is often neglected as a writer. Her poems have not been
neglected, of course, but the personal has often been emphasized
at the expense of the professional. This has happened because she
was a woman, I argue. If this seems a feminist 'bias', many male
critics have been more obsessed with the fact that Dickinson was
a woman than I am. One has called Dickinson 'a private poet
who wrote indefatigably, as some women cook or knit'. Another
claims that 'the eruption of her imagination and poetry followed
when she shifted her passion, with the energy of desperation,
from [the] lost man onto his only possible substitute — the entire
Universe in its Divine aspect'. Recent feminist writers have been
less blinded by conventional stereotypes about women, but sometimes they have risked creating new myths of their own. I have
tried to approach Dickinson as one writer would another, doing

her the professional courtesy of taking the work more seriously than the life. I have not left the life out, but I have only used so much of it as is necessary to understand the poems. Nevertheless, I hope I have created a demythologized, living picture of Dickinson the woman as well as of Dickinson the writer.

I have enjoyed writing this book, perhaps because, like Dickinson, I 'see New Englandly'. It has brought back walking in the blizzard-coated Pelham Hills in men's construction boots from the Springfield Army-Navy store, cycling along back roads during the dog days of high summer past Polish immigrants' farms, and buying half-bushels of Macoun apples near Montague. And I have even enjoyed reading all 1,775 poems, in the Radcliffe Camera during another hot summer when the square outside was occupied by a busking flute-player who rendered the variations on 'La Folia' in the same dragging tempo at two o'clock every afternoon.

To Christopher Britton — a better flute-player — I owe the space of time and the peace of mind to write this book. To my editor, Miriam Kochan, and my publisher, Marion Berghahn, I am indebted for their confidence and encouragement. To my daughter, Kirsten, I am grateful for her false but flattering conviction that two 'Dickensons' must be related, even if one did insist on spelling her name with an 'i'. And to my son, Anders, I give the news that he spent a short time in Amherst as an embryonic recluse, although in a more restricted space than the Homestead afforded.

DONNA DICKENSON
Oxford, May 1985

2

1 Relations

This book will suggest that the personal has been overemphasized in most accounts of Emily Dickinson's life and work, and that the professional has been neglected. In my view the tragedy in Dickinson's story is that she failed to publish — to attain the recognition which has ripened late, if voluptuously. The myths which helped to sell Dickinson's poems to the public after her death presented her as a literary Grandma Moses, a naïve and unprofessional genius. These legends embroidered lavishly on the ironically scanty facts we possess about the personal life of a writer who is known so largely *for* her personal life. It has been estimated that we have only about one-thousandth of all the letters Dickinson received, and one-tenth of those she sent — many of them couched in riddles. It has been said that her biography 'affords about as much material as the experience of some life-termer in a penitentiary'.[1] Rarely has there been a writer about whose private life so little is known.

But no doubt this skimpiness of detail is just what has lent the myths their appeal — and made them conveniently difficult to disprove. The two hoariest bits of literary gossip concern Dickinson's supposed rejection by a mysterious lover and her father's alleged tyranny over her life. They coalesce in the third legend, that of the pitiable recluse who was either jilted or browbeaten into locking herself away from the world. These myths enjoy an ancient lineage and a favoured status in such respectable society as Ted Hughes's 1968 collection of Dickinson's poems or comparatively recent editions of the *Encyclopaedia Brittanica*. Nevertheless, they are almost certainly false, and clearly sexist. Thoreau was also a hermit during part of his life, but no one attributes his reclusion to a domineering mother or an oddly untraceable lady friend. Because Dickinson was a woman, the personal is assumed to have been more important to her than the professional. Nevertheless, there are many proofs that Dickinson regarded herself as a professional poet, not as a genteel spinster who wrote poems to kill the time which other women occupied with theorem painting, *petit point*, or duty calls. (In any case, she would have agreed with

Thoreau that you cannot kill time without injuring eternity.) The clearest indication that she was no Sunday poet lies in the volume of her work: over 300 poems dated to 1862 alone, and a total output of almost 1,800 poems. She revised, made lists of words, experimented with metres, tried to publish, and did all the other things that poets do. In every sense but the success, she was a professional. It is that, and her training at Mount Holyoke Seminary that the determined and diligent may become whatever they want to be, which must have made the lack of recognition hard to bear. The cascade of posthumous fame makes us forget that she was a failure in her own life and terms. Yet she went on writing till her death, and that itself is a sign of a professional attitude.

It may seem odd to begin with an account of Dickinson's family background, when I have just said I intend to play down the personal. There is no denying, however, that the personal makes compulsive reading: the appeal of the myths is understandable, even if a surfeit cloys. And there is no contradiction between recognizing Dickinson as a disciplined professional and admitting that her extraordinary background influenced her. The personal cannot be omitted altogether: what *is* wrong-headed is to let the background obscure the professional achievement. But the background is still necessary, though not sufficient, to an understanding of the poems. This chapter will present the characters in Dickinson's family theatre; the next one will range outside the Homestead to look at the Connecticut River valley culture into which the poet was born in 1830.

Dickinson's family were prominent in Amherst and well-established in the Connecticut valley for generations. Both her father Edward and her brother Austin were referred to as 'squire', without either proletarian irony or Cockney chirpiness. (Later, in my chapter on 'Reclusion', I shall consider the suggestion that Dickinson's self-imposed isolation was somewhat of a slap in the face for her socially active family, rather than an expression of dutiful daughterliness.) Although the poem 'I'm Nobody' is probably about Dickinson's inability to achieve recognition as a poet, it can plausibly be read as a wry comment on the genteel Boosterism of the Dickinsons:

I'm Nobody! Who are you?
Are you Nobody – Too?
Then there's a pair of us?
Don't tell! They'd advertise – you know!

How dreary – to be Somebody!
How public – like a Frog –
To tell one's name – the livelong June –
To an admiring Bog!   (288, *c*. 1861)

But Edward and Austin were repairing ancestral fortunes which had fallen in the days of Emily's grandfather, Samuel Fowler Dickinson. The Dickinsons arrived with John Winthrop in 1630 and settled in Wethersfield, Connecticut. In nearby Avon, down a lane allowed to revert to a straggly track after the land had been exhausted and the forest left to return, I once saw a tombstone with this inscription:

Uncertain life, how swift it flies –
Dream of an hour, how brief our bloom.
Like the gay verdure, soon we rise,
Cut down 'ere night to fill the tomb.

The grave belonged to Libby Dickinson, 1798–1818. By the turn of the nineteenth century there were Dickinsons all over the Connecticut valley, and in the 1880s a family historian wrote that the Amherst and Hadley specimens 'threatened to choke out all other forms of vegetation'.[2] This Massachusetts branch was founded in 1659, when some sixty families settled in Hadley under Nathaniel Dickinson's leadership after a church schism. Nathaniel was one of the few men entrusted with knowledge of the secret hiding-place — presumably after West Rock in New Haven — of the regicides Goffe and Whalley. Dickinsons fought in scores among the Minutemen, and Emily's great-great-great-grandfather is recorded as warring against the Indians at Deerfield after the massacre of 1704.

Although the Dickinsons belonged to a New England aristocracy, they were impoverished nobility by the time Emily's father, Edward, took over the law practice from his father, Samuel Fowler Dickinson (1770–1835). 'Squire Fowler' — who shared

5

the honorific which seems so incongruous for descendants of the radical sects and the Minutemen — began life as a classical scholar, during the great era of learning in the northeast, when the countryside was burgeoning with new Corinths, Troys, and Romes. The law practice which he later founded was said to do more business than that transacted by all the county's remaining lawyers put together. But he died in obscurity and near-bankruptcy, having been forced to leave Amherst and migrate west when he threw too much of his own capital into the founding of the college. In his determination to establish a rival college which might counteract the liberal unitarianism of Harvard — which retaliated by branding Amherst College a 'priest factory' — he neglected his firm, exhausted his own horses in drawing brick for the college buildings, and insisted that his wife board the labourers, whom he paid out of his own pocket. He seems to have been as devoted to his cause as Emily was to hers, the writing — and as unconcerned with the embarrassing consequences for his family or his own reputation. The president of Amherst College, Edward Hitchcock, later described him as 'one of the most industrious and persevering men that I ever saw . . . a man of very decided religious principles, and when satisfied that he was in the path of duty, his face was as a flint, and he reminded one of the early Puritans'.[3]

Samuel Fowler Dickinson had the Yankee energy as well — the vigour which has been described as destructive when turned in on itself, but essential to the wresting of a stingy living from the granite-choked soil. His daughter described him in these terms:

He allowed himself but four hours of sleep, studying and reading until midnight, and rising at four o'clock he often walked to Pelham [several miles east of Amherst, and set in low mountains] or some other town before breakfast. Going to court at Northampton, he would catch up his green bag and walk the whole seven miles. 'I cannot wait to ride', he would say to those who suggested that many horses in his stable would be idle, and he outwalked the stage, with its four-in-hand, to Northampton. Bread, cheese and coffee, apples and old cider before breakfast were almost his sole diet.[4]

It was not luxurious living which impoverished him and drove him from his much-loved Amherst to the Cincinnati wilds scorned by literate New Englanders.

This frugality he extended to the education of his daughters, not long after Wollstonecraft had despaired that Englishwomen were taught nothing beyond how to excite male sexuality. 'A good husbandman will also educate well his daughters', he said in his last speech before leaving Amherst. Although he viewed women as occupying a separate place in society, he was sincere in his belief that it should be separate but equal — a shibboleth to us, but a meaningful principle to him and to the other founders of the town academy and college. Girls were to be educated in the 'useful' sciences, but here he included everything pertaining to a 'good English education' (which Wollstonecraft would have found ironic) — 'a thorough knowledge of our own language, geography, history, mathematics, and natural philosophy'. What Emily studied at Amherst Academy forms an impressive list of subjects — algebra, chemistry, natural theology, church history, anatomy, astronomy, geology, logic, Latin, New Testament Greek, arithmetic, geography, ancient history, grammar and composition. The admission which girl pupils at the Academy also enjoyed to lectures at the College — long before any English university opened its portals to women — may have been due in some measure to her grandfather's views. Yankee frugality and godliness, rather than any conscious feminism, dictated his views on female education: 'The female mind, so sensitive, so capable of improvement, should not be neglected . . . God hath designed nothing in vain.'[5]

It is a truism that these reasonably enlightened views were not passed on to Samuel's son Edward (1803–74), whose opinions about women's proper station might seem to lend initial support to the story of the tyrannical father. Although his letters show that he valued his daughters' education as much as his son's, he also denounced the early suffragists as 'a class of females . . . some sentimental, some belligerent, some fist-shakers, some scolds'. In a letter written in 1826 to his future wife, Emily Norcross, he described his pride at meeting a native New England 'authoress' but cautioned her against attempting any similar tricks: cleverness in women did not make for domestic harmony. (Perhaps this is one reason why his daughter, like Jane Austen, generally hid her writing from her family: her sister Lavinia was stunned to discover the size of her manuscript collection after she died.) From this premature display of paterfamilial authority to the dour sternness displayed in the portrait of the older Dickinson — pillar of the college, wealthy lawyer and public man — seems no distance at all. It might be tempting to believe that this man could have occasioned his daughter's withdrawal from the world, when he supposedly chastised her for staying out past her curfew and she immediately countered that she would never emerge from his house again.[6] It is true enough that Emily wrote in 1866 'I do not cross my Father's ground to any house in town' — but was this necessarily her father's doing?

There are many indications that in his youth, at least, Edward Dickinson was quite a lively soul, if not a gay blade. (It should also be noted that her sister and many of her contemporaries described Emily as naturally cheerful, another fact the posthumous myths ignore.) At Yale Edward Dickinson wrote original poems in his senior year-book, when most of his peers were content to copy out enlightening sentiments by Burns, Shakespeare or Thomson. His friends said that he was possessed of 'natural liveliness and universal good nature'. In his letters to his fiancée he strayed beyond moral homilies into enthusiastic expressions of solidarity with the Greek independence fighters. Later in life he was so moved by a marvellous display of the northern lights that he rang the church bells to summon the whole of Amherst. When he was young, he described himself in these terms:

> I am naturally quick and ardent in my feelings, easily excited, though not so easily provoked — decided in my opinions — determined in accomplishing whatever I undertake — hard to be persuaded that I am wrong when I have once formed an opinion upon reflection — sometimes unyielding and obstinate — rather particular — have a little personal irritability in my constitution . . . . [7]

Biographers of Emily Dickinson have taken rather unfair advantage of these lines, written as part of a character-guessing game and in the spirit of fun. In any case, a genuine tyrant might not be so hard on himself.

But it may well be that the natural ardour of Edward Dickinson's character hardened with age and responsibility. He had to grow up quickly, rebuilding the family firm after his father's débâcle, and the early years of his marriage were marked by enduring foreclosure on his mortgage, sharing a rented house with another family, and having to cram himself, his wife and his growing brood into two rooms. He had not wanted to return to Amherst from Yale in the first place, just as his son Austin was depressed in his turn by how strait and narrow was the predetermined path to squiredom in a country town. (It is interesting to note that Emily typically referred to men's responsibilities with pity, not with envy. Hawthorne in the custom-house at Salem, Thoreau doing odd jobs for Emerson, Melville scribbling away in the records office — all might have envied her, confining though her life was in other respects.)[8] When Austin left home to teach — and to put off the day when he would have to join his father's practice — Emily wrote to him: 'We don't have many jokes now, it is pretty much all sobriety, and we do not have much poetry, Father having made up his mind that it's pretty much all real life.' Most critics have read this as sad for Emily, but it is quite pathetic for her father, too, of course. Later in the mid-1860s, she wrote to Joseph Lyman, a friend of her youth:

My father seems to me often the oldest and oddest sort of foreigner. Sometimes I say something and he stares in a curious sort of bewilderment, though I speak a thought quite as old as his daughter ... Father says in fugitive moments when he forgets the barrister and lapses into the man, says that his life has been passed in a wilderness or on an island — of late he says on an island. And so it is, for in the morning I hear his voice and methinks it comes from afar and has a sea tone and there is a hum of hoarseness about it and a suggestion of remoteness as far as the isle of Juan Fernandez.

Emily Dickinson's mother, Emily Norcross Dickinson (1804–82), has suffered her share of victimization from the myth-makers, too. The stories have been of a different sort from the ogre legends about Edward Dickinson, but perhaps even more unflattering — although with even less basis in fact. Three contradictory accounts emerge: the ineffectual mother, the over-protective mother, and the malevolent wicked-stepmother figure straight from 'Hansel and Gretel'. The first stereotype seems to date from her later life, when she was lingering in illness and might perhaps have been expected to be released from any further duties towards her grown-up children. It was supported by Austin's mistress, Mabel Loomis Todd, who described Emily Norcross Dickinson as a 'meek little thing'. But Todd — herself a flamboyant figure — only knew Mrs Dickinson as a house-bound invalid. More telling, perhaps, are Dickinson's own comments on her mother. Much has been made of her claim in a letter to the literary critic Thomas Wentworth Higginson that 'I never had a mother. I suppose a mother is one to whom you hurry when you are troubled'. She also asserted that her father took her mother's place in her life — with the implication that her father's forbidding manner and business preoccupations left her totally orphaned. 'I always ran Home to Awe when a child, if anything befell me. He was an awful Mother, but I liked him better than none.' She also complained to Higginson that her mother 'did not care for Thought'.

These rather cruel remarks might simply be dismissed as posing, to which Austin said his sister was prone. Dickinson might well have put on airs to impress a Boston literary lion, as well known in his time as Hawthorne. But there remains the question of why she chose this particular pose. Some writers have offered psychoanalytical explanations, and this brings us to the other two stock villainesses of Freudian myth, the dominating mother and the malevolent mother. Of course psychoanalytical explanations need not depend on these anti-female stereotypes. A psychoanalytically orientated feminist writer believes that Dickinson had to reject her perfectly normal, nurturing mother in order to allay her own guilt at choosing the markedly unfeminine role of poet.[9] Other writers have argued that Mrs Dickinson *invited* her daughter's rejection because she was too protective a mother. Clearly this contradicts Dickinson's own complaints about her mother's neglect and suggests that mothers always lose; but it accords with some second-hand evidence, although that testimony may be debatable. Millicent Todd Bingham, Mabel Todd's daughter and the editor of the hidden cache of Dickinson poems which appeared in 1945, describes Mrs Dickinson as a fussy mother, always hovering round her children. But what is the source of this information? It must have come from Todd, but she also supported the first, 'ineffectual' image of Mrs

Dickinson. This disparity suggests one good reason for ignoring the myths about Dickinson's background: they often contradict each other.

The third version of the mother myths — the nasty stepmother — accords with neither the first nor the second. In this image,[10] which is largely based on a chauvinist reading of the available psychological evidence, Mrs Dickinson emerges as a lifelong hypochondriac, a house-proud fanatic, a demanding harpy, and a woman obsessed with her own death. If Dickinson had had a 'proper mother', and not this strolling catalogue of maternal inadequacy, she would have become a 'proper woman', not the severely unbalanced recluse she turned out to be — or so this view claims. Probably she would have had nothing to do with poetry, but then perhaps that is unnatural for a 'proper woman'. Do normal women only drift into poetry if they suffer loss? This comes round to Ted Hughes's view that Dickinson only became a poet because of blighted love: '. . . the eruption of her imagination and poetry followed when she shifted her passion, with the energy of desperation, from [the] lost man onto his only possible substitute — the Universe in its Divine aspect'.[11] Clearly this implies that satisfied, 'normal' women are unlikely to become great poets, and indeed James Reeves's introduction to his *Selected Poems of Emily Dickinson* makes bold to suggest that a woman poet might be a contradiction in terms. In an odd way the feminist view of Dickinson's relations with her mother accepts Reeves's bifurcation. Emily Dickinson *had* a proper mother, in this theory, but had to reject the womanliness her mother embodied, since 'woman' and 'poet' do not mesh.

We are back to my initial claim: that over-emphasis on the personal details of Emily Dickinson's life impedes our understanding of her as a professional poet. The accounts of her relationship with her mother are at odds; the contending myths jostle. It is fruitless to take them any further; what do the poems say? The orphan theme comes out in Dickinson's writing, true enough:

A loss of something ever felt I –
The first that I could recollect
Bereft I was – of what I know not . . .   (959, *c*. 1864)

11

But there is no more reason to suppose that this proves Dickinson 'never had a mother' than that Wordsworth literally emerged from his mother's womb 'trailing clouds of glory'. This Romantic theme of loss was a standard poetic subject, and Dickinson tried them all: death, grief, loss, childhood memories, sunset, God. How else was she to wrest a lifetime's work from the pebbly thin soil of her dull life?

Dickinson normally adopts the first person in her poems, but this does not mean that everything this 'I' says or feels represents her own words or emotions, any more than putting the authorial 'I' in Esther Summerson's mouth meant that Dickens secretly wanted to be a woman. Emily's sister Vinnie (1833–99) made this clear in her vain attempt to scythe down the myths which had grown lustily even in the nine years between the first book of Emily's poems and Vinnie's death: 'Her intense verses were no more personal experiences than Shakespeare's tragedies, or Mrs Browning's minor-key pictures'. Along with the disparaging comments on her mother in her letters to Higginson, Emily warned him that 'When I state myself, as the Representative of the Verse–it does not mean–me–but a supposed person'. We may have cause to doubt her own attempts at myth-making about her mother in her letters, but this businesslike declaration has no reason to pose.

In any case, only very young or very poor writers make everything in their work autobiographical. And only equally naïve readers assume that writers can only express what they have experienced directly. Some psychoanalytical writers on Dickinson have made this assumption:

> It has been argued that the 'I' in Emily Dickinson's poems does not refer to herself but, as she said, to a 'supposed person'. . . . We must ask ourselves whether anyone, even a poet, can portray a feeling state that he has not himself undergone. And if one grant that this is possible, what could possibly motivate a person to attempt to express what he never felt?[12]

But of course that is exactly the sort of self-imposed puzzle which a writer sets out to solve, much as a composer bounds himself in with restrictions to compose a fugue. Villon had not actually been hanged, needless to say, when he wrote the 'Ballade des pendus', though he had been sentenced and reprieved. There was that much basis in experience for the poem but not the literal basis of the sort postulated in this quotation. Dickinson left Amherst for more than very short visits only two or three times in her life and never for as much as a year. Yet she begins poem 609 with the line 'I Years had been from Home'. She knew how to keep fact and fiction in separate compartments: in a letter of 1877 which discusses Austin and Sue's unhappy marriage, she remarks, 'Sorrow is unsafe when it is real sorrow'. All this suggests that we do not need to look for a basis in literal experience to understand why Dickinson took up the orphan theme.

The verdict on Emily Norcross Dickinson must be 'not proven' on all three incompatible counts — neglect, over-protection, and wilful harm. The facts behind the myths are inadequate for proof, as we might expect: she was a denizen of the private domain, a family woman. The details about her husband's life and personality are more solid and numerous, since he was very much the public man: but even these facts have been twisted or ignored by determined legend-seekers. All we can know about Emily Norcross Dickinson is that she performed the normal duties of a 'squire's' wife: she was active in the church, gave receptions for the college, served on the cattle show committee, and won prizes for her cookery and produce. If she did suffer from 'complaints' — and nineteenth-century women were expected to, unaware as they were that the twentieth century would turn around and mock them for hypochondria — these duties cannot have been easy to perform. If she had a husband who was rather short of social graces, they would have been harder still. It may well be that she was patronized by her husband from courtship onwards, judging from the moral lectures he offered her, and perhaps Emily scorned her for it. But the worst crime Mrs Dickinson seems to have committed is distance — and the Dickinson family as a whole was a confederation of independent states. Vinnie said that her family lived together 'like friendly and absolute monarchs, each in his own domain'. After her mother's long decline and her death, Emily wrote, 'We were never intimate Mother and children while she was our Mother – but mines in the same Ground meet by tunnelling, and when she became our Child, the Affection came'.

The Dickinsons were a clannish family, too, with a fair degree of snobbery towards outsiders. Perhaps it is indicative that the family did not even attend Austin's wedding to Susan Gilbert, although they would only have had to cross the state boundary. Emily's dismissive comments towards her mother in the 1862 letter to Higginson almost seem to reflect the typical Dickinson distrust and scorn of outsiders. After all, Emily Norcross had only become a Dickinson by marriage! But it was with her brother (William) Austin (1829–95) that Emily served her apprenticeship in shutting out the world. This isolation, which will be explored at greater length in chapter four, was to produce poems like this:

> The Soul selects her own Society –
> Then – shuts the Door –
> To her divine Majesty –
> Present no more –
>
> Unmoved – she notes the Chariots – pausing –
> At her low Gate –
> Unmoved – an Emperor be kneeling
> Upon her Mat –
>
> I've known her – from an ample Nation
> Choose One –
> Then – close the Valves of her attention –
> Like Stone –   (303, *c*. 1862)

As children Austin and Emily — with Vinnie as a barely tolerated younger intruder — formed a small coven against their preoccupied and often strict parents. They traded jokes and banter, talked into the night 'upon the kitchen stone hearth, when the just are fast asleep', and competed in poetic composition. Emily felt quite poignantly the separation which adulthood entailed, expressing her sorrow in the language of Dickinson exclusiveness: 'I think we miss each other more every day that we grow older, for we're all unlike most everyone'. These same not entirely attractive sentiments fill this poem:

I know lives, I could miss
Without a Misery –
Others – whose instant's wanting –
Would be Eternity –

The last – a scanty Number –
'Twould scarcely fill a Two –
The first – a Gnat's Horizon
Could easily outgrow –   (372, *c*. 1862)

Naturally it is tempting to speculate on the composition of this
élite: the one definite, and the other who barely makes up the
'Two'. I have said that I find such speculation pointless, but so
compulsive is Dickinson gossip that it might be permissible to
indulge in it just this once. It seems to me that the great unrequited love of Dickinson's life — if she had one — was Austin.
She was greatly distressed at the time of Austin's engagement to
Susan Gilbert, her great friend, when she might have been
expected to be pleased. She wrote letters to Sue deprecating
marriage, and to Austin comparing brother and sister to two
lovers in a Hawthorne story. The oddest bit of 'proof' is this
poem, which can only be addressed to someone who shared her
surname and features:

The face I carry with me – last
When I go out of Time –
To take my Rank – by – in the West –
That face – will just be thine –

I'll hand it to the Angel –
That – Sir – was my Degree –
In Kingdoms – you have heard the Raised –
Refer to – possibly.

He'll take it – scan it – step aside –
Return – with such a crown
As Gabriel – never capered at –
And beg me put it on –

And then – he'll turn me round and round –
To an admiring sky –
As one that bore her Master's name –
Sufficient Royalty!   (336, *c.* 1862)

The reference to 'Master' in the final stanza of this puzzling poem echoes the better-known trio of letters to an unknown 'Master', and I shall come on to these at the end of this chapter, when I consider other contenders in the lover myth. I still believe that it *is* a myth, and a patronizing one. Not only does it assume that all normal women need male lovers, and that Dickinson went insane because she lacked one: it also implies that women are only capable of going mad with masculine help. In the end I believe that both this poem and others apparently dedicated to an unknown lover can be explained in other, better ways. Some of the poems are androgynous: it is only convention which leads us to regard their subjects as men, rather than grammar. Indeed, Dickinson left a duplicate of 'Going to Him! – happy letter!' — acceptably heterosexual, and published in 1891 — which begins 'Going to Her – happy letter!' — ignored until 1955. It has been suggested that Dickinson was a lesbian, but although I do not rule any of these possibilities out of court, I feel that speculation about a mysterious female lover is no more fruitful that surmises about the male equivalent. Other poems do seem definitely to be addressed to a male subject, but they could either be fantasies — normal enough, and not necessarily indications of madness — or experiments using a conventional poetic theme. As Robert Frost has said, poets do not need to go to Niagara if they wish to portray the force of falling water. Poets write all sorts of exercises to keep in trim: sometimes the exercises turn out to be good poems in themselves, sometimes not. It is no more puzzling when women poets choose love as the subject of an exercise than when they choose daffodils or sunsets, but daffodils and sunsets are not the stuff of literary gossip.

After this foray into speculation about Dickinson's personal life, I must return to my sketch of Austin. It is impossible to escape from titillating scandal altogether in discussing him, however, since that is what he is often remembered for — the affair he began in his fifties with Mabel Loomis Todd, the young wife of an astronomy lecturer at Amherst College, where he was treasurer.

16

Generally critical opinion has supported Austin and castigated his wife Sue, in the tediously unsurprising way of the world. Of course it is true that we would not have Emily Dickinson's poems if Austin had not crossed his 'Rubicon' with Todd — as he laconically noted the day of their probable first assignation in his diary. Todd edited some 600 of the poems after Emily's death, reopened the poet's old fruitless correspondence with Higginson, and tramped round publishers' offices in Boston at the literary man's direction. With her daughter, Millicent Todd Bingham, she brought another 600 poems to light at the end of her life, in circumstances which will be described in chapter 6. But Todd and Austin have come across almost wholly favourably in the myths — probably because of the able attack on Susan and her daughter, Martha Dickinson Bianchi, which Bingham mounted. As with the other legends surrounding Dickinson, some debunking is required.

Austin was a glittering figure in Amherst, the well-to-do squire's son who wore a yellow planter's hat and lavender trousers at town meetings, drove fine horses, and entertained Emerson at his home. This glamour, combined with his destruction of his wife's letters to him and Bingham's hostility towards Sue, has made it difficult for us to see his marriage in any but a one-sided perspective. Susan Gilbert Dickinson, a cultivated and intelligent woman who kept something of a salon in Amherst, is typically vilified or ignored in accounts of Dickinson's life. Yet Sue was the first person to whom Emily showed her poems, and she offered more sagacious comments than Higginson, judging from the beneficial revision which Dickinson undertook on 'Safe in their Alabaster Chambers' after sounding Sue's opinion. Later in her life Emily said to Sue, 'With the exception of Shakespeare, you have told me of more knowledge than anyone living – To say that sincerely is strange praise'. (Strange indeed, not least because it implies Shakespeare was alive in the nineteenth century! — but perhaps he was to Dickinson, in her inward-turned world.) None of Sue's letters survive, but we have enough of Austin's early ones to her to know that he made narcissistic demands on her sympathy without offering too much in return. Perhaps he was rather used to considerable adulation from Emily, who viewed it as her life's work 'to make everything pleasant for Father and Austin'. (He enjoyed the same support from Vinnie during the Todd affair: perhaps the old Dickinson exclusiveness still shut Sue out even after thirty years of marriage.) After a very minor illness in 1850, Austin was going on to Sue at length about his moods brought on by 'severe Physical Pain' and of his 'exceeding discomfort and gloom'. In the same letter he complained further, 'I never *did*, and don't *now think*, we understand each other'. Yet he married her, and she bore him three children, one in her forties. This youngest child, (Thomas) Gilbert, died at the age of eight in 1883. Austin was thunderstruck, by all accounts, but we hear little of Sue's grief. At least Austin already had Todd to comfort him — and it was as Sue's acquaintance that Todd had first entered their house, and as their elder son Ned's heart-throb that she first demonstrated her gratitude to Sue. Ned gave her up — she was of course a married woman, and Amherst a small town — but Austin carried on his affair with her until his death in 1895. Todd's husband, David, may have been too much in awe of Austin's position as college treasurer to object, and Sue was powerless. In a small New England town, this affair would have been a constant humiliation for Sue, as was the entrusting of Emily's poems — which Sue had first read when Todd was a baby — to her husband's mistress for publication. Perhaps she thought back to the letter Emily had written her before her marriage to Austin: 'The new bride must look on our single lives as dull, but the neglected wife must envy our freedom'.

Whatever the rights and wrongs of the affair, it has added one more salacious element to the Dickinson legend. Indeed, strained relations between the Evergreens — Austin and Sue's home — and the Homestead next door, where Emily and Lavinia lived, may have contributed to the drying-up of exuberance which Dickinson's later poems are sometimes said to show. The feud continued down to Sue's and Mabel's daughters, and a major cause of the rancour was a lawsuit which Todd brought against Lavinia. In her account of the poems' publication, Millicent Todd Bingham reproduces her mother's comment on Vinnie: 'A brilliant exponent of ancient wit and comment not involving any superfluous love for one's fellow men'.[13] Actually this description might have suited all three Dickinsons: although a budding public figure, Austin was notably unmoved by the great causes of his day, such as abolition. He engaged in the practice permitted in the Union conscription statutes but forbidden in the less populous South — buying a substitute to take his place in the Civil War. And Emily was no great friend to the common people:

> The Popular Heart is a Cannon first –
> Subsequent a Drum –
> Bells for an Auxiliary
> And an Afterword of Rum –
>
> Not a Tomorrow to know its name
> Nor a Past to share –
> Ditches for Realms and a Trip to Jail
> For a Souvenir –   (1226, *c.* 1872)

When Austin was away teaching in Boston, Emily mocked his pupils' Irish background in her letters to him and despaired of the time he was wasting on 'these useless boys'. This family pattern of obsession with privacy and rather self-centred un-worldliness continued in Vinnie. By the time Mabel Todd knew her, she was making her calls at night in order to avoid being seen. Although she and Emily lived together for over fifty years, she had no idea of the extent of her sister's output. When asked whether she had ever studied her sister's poems, she replied, 'Certainly not. I never looked at Emily's poems except those she herself showed me. Had she wished me to do so, she would have made her wishes known'. In a family whose members kept themselves strictly to themselves — and whose head fed the sparrows from behind a half-closed door so as not to embarrass them — Dickinson's isolation from the world seems almost normal. Indeed, both Austin and Vinnie always maintained they saw nothing strange about it.

What is difficult but important to understand is that the Dickinsons were not a cold family. The emotional range and subtlety of Dickinson's poetry may seem odd mutations in the neat parterres of her family's garden. But the characters of Samuel, Edward, Austin and Vinnie all indicate strong feelings under the faces of flint — making it less surprising that Emily was able to grow such exotic plants in her own high-walled garden. Certainly there was plenty of affection in the family: in Emily's childhood feelings for her brother, the emotion was too intense, if anything. Emily described her love for Vinnie, too, as a 'bond' which was 'early, earnest, indissoluble. Without her life were Fear, and Paradise a cowardice, except for her inciting voice'. Her voice could laugh, too: there is an account of Vinnie giving forth with uproarious imitations and witticisms over lunch at the Evergreens, until Austin stopped the fun by rapping on the ceiling from his bed upstairs!

Although Emily described Vinnie as the household 'Soldier and Angel', brandishing 'a drawn sword in behalf of Eden', she was rather prone to patronize her, as she did her mother's 'Distaste for Thought'. She claimed that Vinnie was 'happy with her duties, her pussies, and her posies'. And at least in Vinnie's version of who did what chores, Emily managed to palm off most of the errands and the heavy work — including double-digging the garden. (In 1860 the Dickinsons were listed in the census as having only one servant for a twelve-room house. Later up to three were employed, but this did not excuse the daughters of the house from considerable drudgery. Perhaps Emily's seclusion was simply the only way she could manage to have any time left for writing after the household duties had been completed.) But Emily wrote this comment, too, during the winter when Vinnie left home to take care of an aunt in Boston: 'I would like more sisters, that the taking out of one, might not leave such stillness. Vinnie has been all, so long, I feel the oddest fright at parting with her for an hour, lest a storm arise, and I go unsheltered'. When a disaster did occur — a fire in the nearby centre of Amherst — the 48-year-old Emily was touchingly glad of her younger sister's attempt to protect her:

We were waked by the ticking of the bells – the bells tick in Amherst for a fire, to tell the firemen.

I sprang to the window, and each side of the curtain saw that awful sun. The moon was shining high at the time, and the birds singing like trumpets.

Vinnie came soft as a moccasin, 'Don't be afraid, Emily, it is only the fourth of July'.

I did not tell her that I saw it, for I thought that if she felt it best to deceive, it must be that it was . . . .

And so much lighter than day was it, that I saw a caterpillar measure a leaf far down in the orchard; and Vinnie kept saying bravely, 'It's only the fourth of July.' . . .

At seven people came in to tell us that the fire was stopped, stopped by throwing sound houses in as one fills a well . . . .

Vinnie's 'only the fourth of July' I shall always remember. I think she will tell us so when we die, to keep us from being afraid.

It was Vinnie's contention that Emily never had a lover, and given the sisters' closeness, it might be simplest to believe her. But Vinnie did also make some outlandish claims, such as her statement that neither she nor Emily ever married for fear of displeasing their father, even after his death. It is now time to give the mysterious lover thesis fuller scrutiny, if only to clear it out of the way before treating more serious matters in later chapters.

As with the other myths, the romantic theses — for they are many — often contradict each other. Hughes claimed that Dickinson became a poet as a result of *abandonment* by the unidentified lover. Not only does this view make the professional depend entirely on the personal, and both God and poetry second-rate substitutes for a husband; it contradicts another common form of the romantic thesis. This is the claim that it was because Dickinson *had* a romance of a reasonably successful nature that she became a great poet: 'Most probably her poems would not have amounted to much if the author had not finally had her own romance, enabling her to fulfill herself like any other woman.'[14] This position is taken by another male poet, John Crowe Ransom. But the only moderately well-documented romance in Dickinson's life — and the only one which 'amounted to much' — was with an older widower, Judge Otis Lord. This attachment was serious enough for Vinnie to remark 'to take to Judge Lord' when she placed heliotropes in her dead sister's hands before the coffin was closed. But Judge Lord came late into Dickinson's life: the 'romance' only bloomed when she was in her late forties, and he died in 1884, two years before her death at the age of fifty-five. Clearly this cannot be the love which is claimed to have produced the great poetry of her thirties. What other contenders are there?

By the 1930s there were already so many identifications of the mysterious lover that not all could possibly be true. Some were particularly unbelievable, such as the legend that Dickinson met a man in Washington to whom her father took a high-handed dislike, that this would-be lover died of grief, and that Emily never knew where his body lay. Since that time there have been even more guesses, including the lesbian speculations about Dickinson's friend, Kate Scott Anthon. Despite her later seclusion, Dickinson had a reasonably wide acquaintance in her youth: she attended taffy-pulls, huckleberrying excursions, and sleigh-ride parties like any other New England girl of her time. In addition she was armed with an arsenal of cousins and school-masters, many of whom have been included in the guessing game. But the two front runners are generally agreed to be Charles Wadsworth, a Philadelphia clergyman, and Samuel Bowles, the editor of the *Springfield Republican* and a family friend. Both were married men, which provides all the necessary explanation for Dickinson's lifelong regrets, to determined proponents of the lover thesis.

Wadsworth was a Presbyterian minister with a considerable reputation as a public speaker. On one of the two trips away from Amherst which Dickinson made in her lifetime — the other was to an eye specialist in Boston — she heard his sermons, and they may have met, although there is no record of it. Whether or not they met at this time, in 1855, it is known that Wadsworth visited the Homestead in 1860 and in 1880, possibly also in 1861. This was scant opportunity for romance, and it is rather amusing that one of the Wadsworth camp should assert that it is very revealing that Dickinson pinned so much hope on a man whom she had seen no more than two or three times.[15] Occam's Razor would suggest that it might be simpler to rule Wadsworth out altogether as a lover.

Dickinson saw a great deal more of Bowles, and did indeed pin hopes on him — but as a publisher rather than a lover. It is true that even after she was steeped so deep in reclusion as to require most friends to speak to her from behind a half-closed door, Bowles was able to woo her out of her room by standing at the foot of the stairs and shouting, 'Emily, you rascal! Come down here!' But he was of the wrong background and marital status for romance, and what passion she poured into the 'affair' was a fervent but misguided hope that Bowles would help her to literary success. I shall detail in chapter 6 the very limited amount of help he did give her, and the rather greater quantity of condescension with which he treated her writing.

The more implicating evidence against Bowles on the 'affair' charge is quite harmless under cross-examination. It is said that Bowles became a familiar in the Dickinson circle through a supposed affair with Dickinson's sister-in-law, Sue, although he was also a friend of Edward Dickinson. Certainly there is evidence that Bowles enjoyed the company of witty bluestockings like both Sue and Emily,[16] but the 'proof' of a liaison with Sue is an interview which Millicent Todd Bingham conducted with a retired lecturer from nearby Smith College in 1934. Bingham had every reason to besmirch Sue's name posthumously, and the lecturer only arrived at Smith in 1884, after Bowles's death. In any case, an affair with one Dickinson woman would not necessarily prove a liaison with another: perhaps it would make it *less* likely, in that strict and involuted family.

The real source of the lover myth — and the identification with Bowles — is a story by Dickinson's childhood acquaintance and literary confidante of later life, Helen Hunt Jackson. This tale, 'Esther Wynn's Love Letters', printed in *Scribner's* magazine in 1871, concerned a romance between a spinster poet and a married man. Despite Jackson's own disclaimer that she, if anyone, was the original of the heroine, the *Republican* ran an editorial in 1878, after Bowles's death, conjecturing that Esther was an Amherst recluse who wore nothing but white — like Dickinson. The next week the paper printed a denial that Esther was a Dickinson — which smacks of the time-honoured courtroom technique, introducing inadmissible evidence in the full knowledge that the judge will overrule it and thus enshrine it in the jury's memory. The rival Springfield newspaper, the *Union*, took up the story and stood firm by its claim that Esther 'answers in private to the honored name of Dickinson'.

The 'affair' with Bowles seems to be a figment of small-town imagination, and an infatuation with Wadsworth can only have been superficial. The most controversial form of the lover myth suggests Dickinson's childhood friend, Kate Scott Anthon, as a lesbian lover, and again casts aspersions on Sue as a possible second flame. (Although Austin's affair with Todd is the only documented one, there is an odd lingering tendency to blame Sue as more sinning than sinned against.) I shall not examine the lesbian thesis at any length:[17] it is probably no more specious than the male lover myth, and at least it serves to prod us into distrusting all the stories about lovers of either sex. But if we

23

refuse to believe that there was a great love in Dickinson's life, what do we make of the numerous poems which seem to be written as love lyrics? And how do we account for the famous letters addressed to an unknown 'Master'?

I shall deal with the second question first. There are three 'Master' letters, datable by handwriting (our only clue to the poems' dates too, for the most part) to the late 1850s or early 1860s. Two are written in ink with pencil corrections, and one entirely in pencil: there is considerable doubt that any of them was ever sent. Nevertheless, a great deal has been made of them — perhaps out of all proportion, even compared with the other scant artefacts Dickinson left. But there is no denying that two of the letters, at least, make very upsetting reading — although the most grovelling and desperate is the pencil one, which probably never got beyond the stage of a rough outpouring of feelings. Many writers have dwelt particularly on this letter, however, to the exclusion of the first pen one, which is quite sensible in tone.

With their code references to a pet name (Daisy), their implorings, their metaphors of volcanoes, and their very un-Dickinsonian humility, the Master letters seem to bear out both the madwoman and the jilting myths. It needs to be stressed, however, that most of Dickinson's letters are hyperbolic and fey in tone, even when Dickinson is writing to her feet-on-the-ground corn-chandler uncle. In their verbosity the letters are very different from the laconic poems; Dickinson knew how to keep the personal and the professional separate. The obscurity of the Master letters and others actually refutes the claim that Dickinson used the poems to relieve her personal misery — a claim which in any case depends on what I shall be crude enough to call the Urinal Interpretation of Poetry. Typically Dickinson approached her relationships with a mixture of reserve and intensity. The Master letters are all her letters writ large, and we cannot rule out the possibility of posing, to which Austin said she was prone in her correspondence. One biographer has written:

Of course, the possibility of a pervasive irony throughout all three letters cannot be denied. To what extent was Emily phantasising? daydreaming? imagining the whole thing or wilfully overdramatising it? employing her extraordinary rhetorical powers by way of exploring a realm of experience she had only nibbled at the fringes of?[18]

In any case, the Master letters are only a distasteful side-show unless they have some connection with the show in the main ring—the poems. But if we accept Frost's view of how poems are made, there is no need to suppose they do have any such link. Over and over the reader is struck by the gap between Dickinson's narrow life and the breadth of her poetic imagination. Many readers are troubled by this discrepancy, but the most economical and sure way of proceeding is to concentrate on the poems, not to stretch the life on a Procrustean bed until it fits them. 'We should not be troubled by the refusal of the *life* to explain the *poetry*.'[19] Certainly we should beware the myths, and the commonest myth is probably that of the mysterious lover. But we have seen that that legend has even less basis in fact than the stories circulated about Dickinson's family. Perhaps 'but' is less appropriate than 'and': it is the lack of fact which has allowed speculation to flourish in this medieval manner. 'Where the allurements of romance coincide with a knowledge vacuum, legends flourish. They have flourished, unfortunately, here. . . . The dubious assumption behind it all is that Emily was staking her life on romantic happiness, and, when that failed her, gave up and withdrew.'[20]

Certainly the lover myth rests on the shakiest proofs, and the relevance of the Master letters to the poetry is open to question, even if the Master *was* an unknown lover. All the same, Dickinson wrote many poems about love — by no means her only or even her most common subject, as the critical emphasis on romance in her own life might lead one to think, but nevertheless a theme. How do we explain this, if we renounce the attempt to make the life explain the poetry?

I have already suggested three possible explanations: that some poems are androgynous according to occasion, that some perfectly normal sexual fantasy may come into the matter, and that Dickinson used romance as she would any other stock poetic theme. Indeed, these three points reinforce each other: if love was a bloodless enough theme for Dickinson to trot it out for suitable occasions — and many of her poems were written for known occasions — she must have been using it in an abstract manner.

Dickinson's warning that she uses a persona in the poems bears out this argument, especially because the character she takes on is sometimes male — as in her frequent references to her boyhood. The poem 'Her sweet weight on my heart a night', which has a male speaker, is based on the common ballad theme of the bride who dies young. Nor need the language of marriage in her poems be a literal language. We are very prone to read deliberately abstract references as personal ones, particularly where women poets are concerned. Some critics claim that Dickinson's use of marriage metaphor shows that she sees herself as Christ's bride rather than any man's. Certainly Dickinson knew how to combine both sorts of metaphor:

> The sweetest Heresy received
> That Man and Woman know –
> Each Other's Convert –
> Though the Faith accommodate but Two –
>
> The Churches are so frequent –
> The Ritual so small –
> The Grace so unavoidable –
> To fail – is Infidel –   (387, *c.* 1862)

Whilst the view of Dickinson as Christ's bride risks enshrining another myth — that of the New England nun — it may accord with the salutary fact that Dickinson devotes far more poems to religious themes than to love lyrics.

Similarly, a personal romantic loss is an excessively literal interpretation of Dickinson's recurring subjects of failure, absence, and atonement. The constant theme of loss *could* spring from maternal rejection or a lover's cruelty, but in the absence of any solid proof that such traumas actually occurred, it is better to read the theme as Dickinson's restatement of a standard Romantic idea. Indeed, it is the abstraction of the loss, the impossibility of giving it a definite biographical focus, which makes the poems powerful:

> For each ecstatic instant
> We must an anguish pay
> In keen and quivering ratio
> To the ecstasy . . .   (125, *c.* 1859)

We have no proof that the ecstasy or the anguish are those of
romantic love in this poem; if we did, it would probably cheapen
the poem for us. And it might just as well be the *absence* of a great
love in Dickinson's life which inspired her, just as

> Water, is taught by thirst.
> Land – by the Oceans passed.
> Transport – by throe –
> Peace – by its battles told –
> Love, by Memorial Mold –
> Birds, by the Snow.   (135, *c.* 1861)

But of course this last interpretation would still make the professional skill depend upon the personal failure — a road I have not
taken.

I think we should be able to look Dickinson's poems in the eye:
glancing over to the life instead is a way of avoiding the poems'
intense gaze. We should be able to return the stare of even an
atypically personal poem like this one:

> Rearrange a "Wife's" affection!
> When they dislocate my Brain!
> Amputate my freckled Bosom!
> Make me bearded like a man!
>
> Blush, my spirit, in thy Fastness –
> Blush, my unacknowledged clay –
> Seven years of troth have taught thee
> More than Wifehood ever may!
>
> Love that never leaped its socket –
> Trust entrenched in narrow pain –
> Constancy thro' fire – awarded –
> Anguish – bare of anodyne!

Burden – borne so far triumphant –
None suspect me of the crown,
For I wear the "Thorns" till Sunset –
Then – my Diadem put on.

Big my Secret but it's *bandaged* –
It will never get away
Till the day its weary Keeper
Leads it through the Grave to thee.
                                        (1737, date unknown)

It is just as misguided to shrink from poems like this because we
dislike the lover myth as it is to seek out references to romance
where none exists. What matters is whether or not the poems
work. (I do not think this poem does work, and I doubt it would
have been given so much attention if it were not so titillating.) I
have suggested that, in order to compose poems that did work,
Dickinson practised doing exercises on stock themes, including
love and loss, and generally left the references in her poems
vague. But this abstraction was combined with down-to-earth
language: the most frequent source of images in her vocabulary is
physical science, with housewifery in second place. Against the
heavenly contemplations and the exotic place-names, she sets
workaday words and wry humour. (Her atypical substitution of
trite words and utter seriousness in poem 1737 accounts for its
failure, I think.) This is a frequent practice in New England
writing — Thoreau did the same — and it is now time to discuss
the extent to which Emily Dickinson 'saw New Englandly', to
move out beyond the circle of her family and friends into the
Connecticut valley culture of the mid-nineteenth century.

Notes

1. Rebecca Patterson, *Emily Dickinson's Imagery*, ed. Margaret H. Freeman (Amherst: University of Massachusetts Press, 1979), p. xvi.
2. Quoted in Richard B. Sewall, *The Life of Emily Dickinson* (New York:
Farrar, Straus and Giroux, 1974), vol. 1, p. 18, fn. 2.

3. Ibid., p. 35.
4. Ibid., p. 38, fn.
5. Ibid., p. 37.
6. Albert J. Gelpi (in *Emily Dickinson: The Mind of the Poet*, Cambridge, Mass.: Harvard UP, 1965) dismisses this as one of the sillier legends about Dickinson's dealings with her father. Gelpi is equally curt about Lavinia's claim that neither she nor Emily ever married because they 'feared displeasing Father even after he was gone' (p. 15). One must be careful, however, about believing Vinnie on some matters, such as Emily's happy temperament, and scoffing at her account of others.
7. Sewall, *Life*, vol. 1, p. 50.
8. This is the view of Jane Donohue Eberwein in 'Doing Without: Dickinson as Yankee Woman Poet', in Paul J. Ferlazzo (ed.), *Critical Essays on Emily Dickinson* (Boston: G. K. Hall and Co., 1984).
9. Barbara Antonina Clarke Mossberg, *Emily Dickinson: When a Writer is a Daughter* (Bloomington, Indiana: Indiana UP, 1982).
10. See, for example, Jack Cody, *After Great Pain* (Cambridge, Mass.: Belknap Press, 1971).
11. Ted Hughes, introduction to *Selected Poems of Emily Dickinson*, (London: Faber, 1968), p. 11.
12. Cody, *After Great Pain*, quoted in Ferlazzo, *Critical Essays*, p. 148.
13. Millicent Todd Bingham, *Ancestors' Brocades* (New York: Harper and Bros., 1945), p. 6.
14. John Crowe Ransom, quoted in Sandra M. Gilbert and Susan Gubar, *The Madwoman in the Attic* (New Haven, Conn.: Yale UP, 1979), p. 543.
15. Gelpi, in his otherwise reliable and comprehensive *Mind*.
16. George Merriam's biography of Bowles, quoted in Sewall, *Life*, p. 471, discusses his attachment to 'women of a characteristically New England type . . . fine intellect, an unsparing conscience, and a sensitive nervous organisation; whose minds have a natural bent towards the problems of the soul and the universe; whose energies, lacking the outlet which business and public affairs give to their brothers, are constantly turned back upon the interior life'. This description has been said to fit Dickinson, of course, but that is no proof of any affair.
17. For this thesis, see Rebecca Patterson, *The Riddle of Emily Dickinson*, 1951.
18. Sewall, *Life*, vol. 2, p. 519.
19. David Porter, quoted in Mossberg, *Daughter*, p. 9.
20. Sewall, *Life*, vol. 2, p. 400.

2 Roots

Here where the wind is always north-north-east
And children learn to walk on frozen toes,
Wonder begets an envy of all those
Who boil elsewhere with such a lyric yeast
Of love that you will hear them at a feast
Where demons would appeal for some repose,
Still clamoring where the chalice overflows
And crying wildest who have drunk the least.

Passion is here a soilure of the wits,
We're told, and Love a cross for them to bear;
Joy shivers in the corner where she knits
And Conscience always has the rocking-chair,
Cheerful as when she tortured into fits
The first cat that was ever killed by Care.[1]

In this sonnet, 'New England', Edwin Arlington Robinson sketches the familiar Yankee portrait, the same face of flint that peers out of Edward Dickinson's picture in his later life. It is a picture of grim temperance and self-denying taciturnity which might seem to explain Emily Dickinson's insistence on the death theme in her poetry and deliberate reclusion in her personal life. Nineteenth-century New England literature was replete with characters whose fictional lives were as deliberately narrow as Dickinson's real one. Sarah Orme Jewett's novel of 1896, *The Country of the Pointed Firs*, includes two farming families who share a small island but have not spoken to each other for three generations. The protagonist in Jewett's story 'The King of Folly Island', George Quint, has vowed never to set foot on any land but his own island after a minor argument with a neighbour — displaying 'the New England will superbly developed, but left no occasion for exercise'.[2] The heroine of Mary E. Wilkins's story 'A New England Nun' has waited fourteen years for her lover to return, but finds that her life has solidified into solitary delicacy of feeling when he does. It has 'turned into a path . . . so straight and unswerving that it could only meet a check at her grave'.[3] Renunciation for its own strong-minded sake, an intense and ascetic form of the death-wish, these are suggested as the motivating forces in the New England spirit. Its fictional representatives

> are documents of the smoldering violence in the New England character, recalling the energy which once subdued a wilderness and settled a land. Now not what they do, but what they essentially are in their passionate commitments — though they have no purpose worthy of commitment — suggests the true measure of their heroism.[4]

Emily Dickinson described herself as having 'an Ancient fashioned Heart' (973) and said 'I see – New Englandly' (285). When her poems were published at last, readers agreed. Samuel Ward, editor of the influential Boston journal *The Dial*, wrote to Dickinson's co-editor Higginson:

> No wonder six editions have been sold, every copy, I should think, to a New Englander. . . . She is the quintessence we all have [sic] who are of the Puritan descent *pur sang*. We came to this country to think our own thoughts with nobody to hinder. . . . We conversed with our own souls till we lost the art of communicating with other people . . . . Such prodigies of shyness do not exist elsewhere. We get it from the English, but the English were not alone in a corner of the world for a hundred and fifty years with no outside interest.[5]

Should we simply accept Dickinson's apparent oddities as intelligible to her time and place, and see her work as conditioned entirely by her bounded life and background?

Certainly we should remember that marriage was by no means so universal in past centuries as it is now, and we should honour the Dickinson family's insistence that there was nothing to indicate madness in the reclusion. But we ought to see Dickinson as original, too, not only as a product of her time. She once protested, 'I. . .never consciously touch a paint mixed by another person'. To see Dickinson as a derivative and particularly quirky representative of an especially eccentric corner of America is to

31

denigrate her work before we even begin to examine it properly. In the first chapter I argued against accepting any of the plentiful stereotypes about Dickinson, and the 'New England nun' is one of these. In any case, the Dickinsons felt themselves to be different from the other Yankee citizens of Amherst. The dour stereotype of Yankee character does not really work for Dickinson. She cultivated rather than repressed her feelings, fairly shouted with exuberance in many of her poems, and enjoyed warm and tender relationships with her family and friends.

> I cannot dance upon my Toes –
> No Man instructed me –
> But oftentimes, among my mind,
> A Glee possesseth me,
>
> That had I Ballet knowledge –
> Would put itself abroad
> In Pirouette to blanch a Troupe –
> Or lay a Prima, mad . . .   (326, *c.* 1862)

Nor was Dickinson an uneducated rural primitive: later in this chapter I shall delineate the extent of her reading and the many resemblances between her and the English Romantics.

In any case, the grey and grim picture of New England is itself a stereotype. If it was ever true — and Robinson was a Maine man, fair enough — it was more applicable to the Puritan period than to the mid-nineteenth century. By then the Calvinist religion had given way to revivalism and the New England small businessman's dominance was weakening with the rise of monopoly capitalism. It was a buoyantly aggressive time of turning outwards, not of reclusion: a period of active social concern, too, whose literary representatives were generally civic-minded men and women — and we have already seen how little civic concern Dickinson possessed. Dickinson *was* very much a Yankee in her verbal frugality and dry wit. But the old Puritan dominance over New England thought and character was being challenged in her time, throwing the old values into doubt. The major contender against the old Calvinism, apart from revivalism, was transcendentalism, and there is a well-documented debate as to whether transcendentalism or Puritanism was the greater influence on Dickinson's work.

If Dickinson was a Puritan — even a throw-back sort of one, as Bowles said her father was 'a Puritan out of time for kinship and appreciation, but exactly in time for example and warning' — it was not because she accepted Calvinist doctrine, but because her mind was imbued with the Protestant ethic and the Puritan emphasis on individual responsibility. Her scepticism about doctrine persisted from her year at Mount Holyoke Seminary (when she was one of the few girls to resist public conversion) to her later life, when she wrote this poem to her nephew Ned:

> The Bible is an antique Volume –
> Written by faded Men
> At the suggestion of Holy Spectres –
> Subjects – Bethlehem –
> Eden – the ancient Homestead –
> Satan – the Brigadier –
> Judas – the Great Defaulter –
> David – the Troubadour –
> Sin – a distinguished Precipice
> Others must resist –
> Boys that "believe" are very lonesome –
> Other Boys are "lost" –
> Had but the Tale a warbling Teller –
> All the Boys would come –
> Orpheus' Sermon captivated –
> It did not condemn –   (1545, *c.* 1882)

The Bible provided Dickinson not with beliefs but with poetic subjects, of which her life was short: hymn metres influenced her style, though she broke their bounds frequently. Beyond these influences, how important was Puritanism to her? I shall examine Dickinson's religion at greater length in chapter 5: for now, I want to concentrate on the Puritan legacy of individual responsibility, which *is* central to Dickinson.

Puritanism minimized the importance of priestly intercession: no one but the believer was responsible for her own salvation. I say 'her' advisedly, because this aspect of Calvinism has sometimes been seen as liberating for women. It is true that the religion's code remained 'He for God only, she for God in Him'. A Puritan marriage manual of 1619 advised that 'Every good woman must suffer herself to be convinced in judgment that she is not her husband's equal'.[6] And some writers hold that the Puritan legacy was different — and grimmer — for Dickinson than it would have been for a male writer:

> Emerson was not raised to celebrate piety, purity, submissiveness and domesticity as divinely commanded attributes of himself. He was not taught that God would punish men who preferred the pen (or the scalpel, or the balance sheet, or anything else) to the broom.[7]

Nevertheless, Puritanism gave women an inner world to conquer, a private realm of equal or greater importance to the masculine public one. A woman was dependent on no one but herself for her own spiritual well-being, and it was by an intense spiritual striving that she was to gain her own salvation. In the seventeenth century the Puritan poet Anne Bradstreet linked this quest to the practice of poetry — and gained some worldly success from it, too. Puritanism made it somewhat easier for a commoner woman to publish: Bradstreet was no Countess of Pembroke. Gaining power by turning inwards — Bradstreet's 'strategy' — may help to explain Dickinson's reclusion. Rather than a sign of lunacy, this intense preoccupation with the private could be a concentration on what is essential for spiritual development.

> Growth of Man – like Growth of Nature –
> Gravitates within –
> Atmosphere, and Sun endorse it –
> But it stir – alone –
>
> Each – its difficult Ideal
> Must achieve – Itself –
> Through the solitary prowess
> Of a Silent Life . . .   (750, *c.* 1863)

'Effort – is the sole condition', this poem continues — another component of Puritan thought and the Protestant ethic. The search for revelation was to be perpetual but not necessarily successful: grace remained in God's keeping, and was unpredictable. Striving and suffering are *necessary* to grace:

> Who never lost, are unprepared
> A Coronet to find!
> Who never thirsted
> Flagons, and Cooling Tamarind! (73, *c.* 1859)

But since suffering and striving may not be *sufficient* for grace, there is an almost Romantic or Existential tendency for them to become ends in themselves. We cannot know whether renunciation will produce salvation: instead it may simply become a habit.

> Art thou the thing I wanted?
> Begone – my Tooth has grown –
> Supply the minor Palate
> That has not starved so long –
> I tell thee while I waited
> The mystery of Food
> Increased till I abjured it
> And dine without like God –
> (1282, 1st version, *c.* 1873)

It was a dismal and lonely version of Puritanism which was left to nineteenth-century New Englanders. Men and women were enjoined to be ceaselessly active in the quest for grace, but there was no surety that grace would be conferred. They would have to look in their own hearts for God rather than to a priestly comforter, but God might be temporarily or permanently absent:

> Prayer is the little implement
> Through which Men reach
> Where Presence – is denied them.
> They fling their Speech
>
> By means of it – in God's ear –
> If then He hear –
> This sums the Apparatus
> Comprised in Prayer – (437, *c.* 1862)

35

Compare Dickinson's deadened scepticism about the efficacy of prayer to Herbert's exuberant confidence:

Prayer, the Church's banquet, Angels' age,
God's breath in man returning to his birth,
The soul in paraphrase, heart in pilgrimage,
The Christian plummet, sounding heaven and earth. . . .
Softness, and peace, and joy, and love, and bliss,
Exalted manna, gladness of the best,
Heaven in ordinary, man well drest,
The milky way, the bird of Paradise,
Church-bells beyond the stars heard, the soul's blood,
The land of spices; something understood.[8]

If God had turned his face from New England Puritans by Dickinson's time, the transcendentalists of her period promised that His reflection might be glimpsed in nature. To be fair, Puritanism had never valued the inner world to the complete exclusion of the outer. It enjoined its faithful to be active in both temporal and spiritual spheres of life — even if it did see women's secular sphere as domestic. Thinkers such as Jonathan Edwards taught that God was pleased by a reasonable amount of rejoicing in earthly things. Puritanism might even have agreed with Dickinson on 'the Fact that Earth is Heaven', although not with her qualifier, 'whether Heaven is Heaven or not' (1408). Transcendentalists certainly did agree that Earth was Heaven, but in a special symbolic sense. 'The universe becomes transparent, and the light of higher laws than its own shines through it', as Emerson said in his essay 'Nature'.

To the transcendentalist, natural beauty and eternal truth exist in a perfect one-to-one correspondence — a linking typical of Romanticism, too. But Dickinson probably first encountered this as a transcendentalist doctrine, through the lectures she attended at Amherst College. The college's first president, Edward Hitchcock, held the view that natural science leads to God — as did the Puritan founders of the Royal Society. On his death, the funeral sermon took up his much-loved theme, that the world is emblematic: 'The elements of nature are a universal alphabet. . . . All science is of God and from God'.

Dickinson often presents nature in this symbolic light, in the best transcendentalist manner. Exactly what nature symbolizes is rarely God, however — whom Dickinson regards as a tyrannical boor — but rather eternity, truth, or immortality. Sometimes the natural is merely a poetic metaphor for the eternal, and the transcendentalism only skin-deep:

> These are the days when birds come back –
> A very few – a Bird or two –
> To take a backward look.
>
> These are the days when skies resume
> The old – old sophistries of June –
> A blue and gold mistake.
>
> Oh fraud that cannot cheat the Bee –
> Almost thy plausibility
> Induces my belief.
>
> Till ranks of seeds their witness bear –
> And softly thro – the altered air
> Hurries a timid leaf.
>
> Oh Sacrament of summer days,
> Oh Last Communion in the Haze –
> Permit a child to join.
>
> Thy sacred emblems to partake –
> Thy consecrated bread to take
> And thine immortal wine!   (130, *c*. 1859)

Often, however, the invisible abstract is inferred from the natural particular in what seems a typically transcendentalist thought-chain:

> The Mountains stood in Haze –
> The Valleys stopped below
> And went or waited as they liked
> The River and the Sky.

At leisure was the Sun –
His interests of Fire
A little from remark withdrawn –
The Twilight spoke the Spire,

So soft upon the Scene
The Act of evening fell
We felt how neighborly a Thing
Was the Invisible.   (1278, *c.* 1873)

But nature is ultimately as indifferent and fickle a companion as grace. In this Dickinson is more the despairing nineteenth-century Puritan than the confident Emersonian.

Summer – we all have seen –
A few of us – believed –
A few – the more aspiring
Unquestionably loved –

But Summer does not care –
She goes her spacious way
As eligible as the moon
To our Temerity –

The Doom to be adored –
The Affluence conferred –
Unknown as to an Ecstasy
The Embryo endowed –   (1386, *c.*1876)

Nature teaches despair and loss as much as it does inspiration and closeness to God.

A light exists in Spring
Not present on the year
At any other period –
When March is scarcely here . . .

Then as Horizons step
Or Noons report away
Without the Formula of sound
It passes and we stay –

A quality of loss
Affecting our Content
As Trade had suddenly encroached
Upon a Sacrament.   (812, *c.* 1864)

Dickinson concludes that 'Nature is a stranger yet;/The ones that cite her most/Have never passed her haunted house,/Nor simplified her ghost'. (1400, *c.* 1877) She made a similar comment in a letter to Higginson the previous year: 'Nature is a Haunted House – but Art – a House that tries to be haunted'. Certainly the complexity of her view of nature finds no echo in Emerson's 'Good-Bye', to which Dickinson had been introduced by her tutor Ben Newton:

> I am going to my own hearth-stone,
> Bosomed in yon green hills alone,
> A secret nook in a pleasant land,
> Whose groves the frolic fairies planned;
> Whose arches green, the livelong day,
> Echo the blackbird's roundelay,
> And vulgar feet have never trod
> A spot that is sacred to thought and God.
>
> O, when I am safe in my sylvan home,
> I tread on the pride of Greece and Rome;
> And when I am stretched beneath the pines,
> Where the evening star so holy shines,
> I laugh at the lore and the pride of man,
> At the sophist schools and the learned clan,
> For what are they all, in their high conceit,
> When man in the bush with God may meet?[9]

Perhaps it is no wonder that Dickinson was affronted rather than flattered when her anonymously printed poem, 'Success is counted sweetest', was attributed to Emerson. Certainly Emerson recognized no kinship between himself and Dickinson, to the extent that he recognized her at all. After reading four of her poems, he wrote,

A Miss Dickenson [sic] writes verses as if threatened with fevers. . . . The few pieces of hers that I have before me are . . . heavy with religious sentiment. She reveals that the old religion of New England has remarkable colors left in it; whilst the heavenly is hellish in her spare lines, the hellish is also made heavenly.[10]

Emerson comes down firmly on the side of Puritanism rather than transcendentalism, then, as the greater influence on Dickinson. Nevertheless, Dickinson had read a great deal of Emerson, disobeying Mount Holyoke's edicts on this as well as in religious matters. She never met him when he stayed with Sue and Austin in 1857, but she called his *Representative Men* 'a little Granite book you can lean on'. The divide between Calvinism and the thought of Concord was by no means complete, in any case. Emerson himself wrote that

Calvinism was still robust and effective on life and character in all the People who surrounded my childhood, and gave a deep religious tinge to manners and conversation. I doubt the race is now extinct, and certainly no sentiment has taken its place on the new generation — none as pervasive and controlling.[11]

And Emerson, too, had his moments of doubt about the amount of comfort a displaced Puritan might expect from nature. The empirical world might be a pointer to permanence, but Emerson was always aware that it was itself transient. It has been said that Dickinson prolonged Emerson's passing doubts into lifelong despair[12] — although this does emphasize the agony in the poems at the expense of the visible ecstasy.

Where Dickinson comes particularly close to Emerson — consciously so — is in her view of the poet's exalted function. This is a Romantic theme as well, of course, but we know that the picture of the drunk-divine poet she paints in this poem was created as a poetic imitation — and gentle parody — of Emerson's essay 'The Poet'.

> I taste a liquor never brewed –
> From Tankards scooped in Pearl –
> Not all the Vats upon the Rhine
> Yield such an Alcohol!

Inebriate of air – am I –
And Debauchee of Dew –
Reeling – thro endless summer days –
From inns of Molten Blue –

When "Landlords" turn the drunken Bee
Out of the Foxglove's door –
When Butterflies – renounce their "drams" –
I shall but drink the more!

Till Seraphs swing their snowy Hats
And Saints – to windows run –
To see the little Tippler
Leaning against the – Sun –   (214, *c.* 1860)

Emerson put it more primly, apparently to Dickinson's amusement:

The poet knows that he speaks adequately, then, only when he speaks somewhat wildly, or with the 'flower of the mind'; not with the intellect used as an organ, but with the intellect released from all service and suffered to take its direction from the celestial life; or as the ancients were wont to express themselves, not with the intellect alone, but with the intellect inebriated by nectar . . . preferably spiritual.

Dickinson's reclusion is also more easily understood in the context of Emerson and Thoreau's glorification of solitude. Romanticism eulogizes solitary reverie too, and Puritanism isolates the individual's own conscience as the locus of salvation, assigning no strength to numbers or institutions. As Thoreau put it, however, 'Any man more right than his neighbors constitutes a majority of one already'.[13] Dickinson expresses the same conviction:

Much Madness is divinest Sense
To a discerning Eye –
Much Sense – the starkest Madness –
'Tis the Majority
In this, as All, prevail –

Assent – and you are sane –
Demur – you're straightway dangerous –
And handled with a Chain –   (435, *c.* 1862)

But neither Dickinson nor Thoreau had the melancholy Romantic love of solitariness: their pleasure in their own company was
just that, at least at the beginning — with a dash of puppy love
for nature. Thoreau's chapter in *Walden* on 'Solitude' includes
these lines:

> Nothing can rightly compel a simple and brave man to a vulgar
> sadness. . . . I have never felt lonesome, or in the least
> oppressed by a sense of solitude, but once, and that was a few
> weeks after I came to the woods, when, for an hour, I doubted
> if the near neighborhood of man was not essential to a serene
> and healthy life. To be alone was something unpleasant. But I
> was at the same time conscious of a slight insanity in my mood,
> and seemed to foresee my recovery.[14]

The 'madness' of reclusion can be divinest sense, and the 'sense'
of living in society madness.

A dry, aphoristic, earth-rooted humour was common to both
Thoreau and Dickinson: an engagingly un-Puritan refusal to take
oneself too seriously, whilst relying on nothing but one's own
judgement. (It has been suggested that Dickinson thus comes to
rely on nothing at all, and that her vision is deeply tragic.[15] If so,
this may underpin the humour rather than contradict it.) More
serious-minded mortals found this flippancy unintelligible and
maddening: Holmes called Thoreau 'a nullifier of civilization
who insisted on nibbling his asparagus at the wrong end', and
Higginson, more damningly, told his wife that Dickinson was
'half-cracked'. Both writers cultivated childlikeness — Thoreau
by refusing to take up any 'respectable' occupation for a Harvard
graduate, Dickinson by remaining all her life in the house which
she referred to not as 'mine' but as 'my father's'. Dickinson's
poetry is full of teasing and riddle, childish inversion, ingenuity in
the original sense, as I shall illustrate in the next chapter.
Emerson despairs when nature refuses to reveal God's plan:
Dickinson sees it as a chance to play hookey from the Almighty,
an opportunity to play one's own games in the exciting dark.

Both she and Thoreau toy with paradox in their writings, enjoying the ambivalence without requiring a resolution of it: both exhibit what Keats termed 'negative capability'. Thoreau eschewed the rationalistic Puritan path to enlightenment in favour of surprise and titillation of the mind. 'Not by constraint or severity shall you have access to true wisdom', he wrote, 'but by abandonment and childlike mirthfulness. If you would know aught, be gay before it'.[16] Hawthorne found Thoreau, true to his principles, to be 'simple and childlike'; Emerson called him 'the boy'. Like Dickinson, he never married. Dickinson repeatedly refers to herself as a child — either boy or girl, indifferently. Both writers are recorded as having been witty and playful in private conversation; both used a laconic Yankee humour in their writings. The myth of Dickinson leaves the laughter out: but she used her lively and telling wit as a weapon against her father's gravity and as a lance against the old Testament figure of God in her poems, where she described herself as a 'satirist'. (118)

It has been said of New Englanders that 'like all people close to the soil, and by education overqualified for the often backbreaking work their livelihoods demanded, they developed a humor that was pithy and ironic'.[17] It is a dry sort of fooling, sere and withered to most American taste. Typically New England jokes concern death, scepticism and silence — all familiar themes in Dickinson's poems. The Vermonter president Calvin Coolidge supposedly replied to a friend who had pointed out that some sheep had been shorn: 'Looks like it from this side'. Another story concerns a traveller who walked past a Yankee farmer who was rocking in his chair on the porch. The stranger made what he thought was a witticism: 'Been rocking like that all your life?' The farmer had his way of dealing with upstarts: 'Not yet', he replied. There is also a story illustrating the laconic Yankee tendency to leave the central bit out whilst maintaining flawless accuracy — a trait which emerges in Dickinson's use of riddle. Farmer Clem asked his neighbour, 'Lem, what did you give your horse when it had colic?' 'Bran mash', Lem answered. Clem went home and returned a week later, complaining, 'Lem, I gave my horse bran mash, and it died.' The reply came, 'So did mine'.[18]

When this bleak 'mortuary merriment'[19] is combined with the equally characteristic Yankee frugality with the verbal currency, it produces aphorism. Thoreau wrote aphoristically: 'We know

43

but few men, a great many coats and breeches'; 'Government is an expedient by which men would fain succeed in letting one another alone'; 'I would rather sit on a pumpkin and have it all to myself than be crowded on a velvet cushion'; 'The mass of men lead lives of quiet desperation'. So did Dickinson: 'Success is counted sweetest/By those who ne'er succeed'; 'Hope is the Thing with Feathers/That perches in the Soul'; 'Water is taught by thirst'; 'None can experience Stint/Who Bounty have not known'; 'A Drunkard cannot meet a Cork/Without a Revery'; 'The Truth I do not dare to know/I muffle with a Jest'.

But if Dickinson used a characteristic New England humour, it was often for the purpose of mocking the received New England canon of virtues. The Vermonter Robert Frost does the same in his poem 'Provide, Provide':

> The witch that came (the withered hag)
> To wash the steps with pail and rag,
> Was once the beauty Abishag,
>
> The picture pride of Hollywood.
> Too many fall from great and good
> For you to doubt the likelihood.
>
> Die early and avoid the fate.
> Or if predestined to die late,
> Make up your mind to die in state,
>
> Make the whole stock exchange your own!
> If need be occupy a throne,
> Where nobody can call *you* crone. . .
>
> Better to go down dignified
> With boughten friendship at your side
> Than none at all. Provide, provide![20]

Good business sense was also a fair target for Dickinson:

> . . . 'Tis sweet to know that stocks will stand
> When we with Daisies lie –
> That Commerce will continue –

And Trades as briskly fly –
It makes the parting tranquil
And keeps the soul serene –
That gentlemen so sprightly
Conduct the pleasing scene!   (54, *c.* 1858)

Nor was this sharp sardonic wit dulled by advancing age and the many losses of her later years. The remark about the drunkard and the cork was written two years before her death, as was the satirical poem which begins:

Of God we ask one favor,
That we may be forgiven –
For what, he is presumed to know –
The Crime, from us, is hidden . . .

(1601, *c.* 1884)

Dickinson's rebellion against God, waged with wit and satire as her arsenal, deepens with age — unusual, when apostasy is generally thought the preserve of the young.

Humour lightens bitterness and enables Dickinson to tangle with mighty subjects whilst avoiding the sentimentality which pervaded Emerson's 'Good-Bye' and oozed from much nineteenth-century poetry. It has been said that 'To grasp the soul at white heat, she needed more than ever the tongs that wit supplied'.[21] Certainly the many references to death would be nothing but lugubrious without the amusement in Dickinson's tone:

Dust is the only Secret –
Death, the only One
You cannot find out all about
In his "native town."

Nobody knew "his Father" –
Never was a Boy –
Hadn't any playmates,
Or "Early history" –

Industrious! Laconic!
Punctual! Sedate!

> Bold as a Brigand!
> Stiller than a Fleet!. . . .   (153, *c.* 1860)

It is humour which prevents this poem from being too Bunyanesque in its heavy allegory:

> I stepped from Plank to Plank
> A slow and cautious way
> The Stars about my Head I felt
> About my feet the Sea.
>
> I knew not but the next
> Would be my final inch –
> This gave me that precarious Gait
> Some call Experience.   (875, *c.* 1864)

Finally, Dickinson's light touch and spareness with words can be charming in themselves:

> To make a prairie it takes a clover and one bee,
> One clover, and a bee,
> And revery.
> The revery alone will do,
> If bees are few.   (1755, date unknown)

Within the grey Puritan dress of taciturnity and dry humour, Dickinson camouflaged a voluptuous body of Romantic themes. She has been called 'a Romantic poet with a Calvinist's sense of things'.[22] As we have seen, transcendentalism mixed the same apparently clashing colours, but Dickinson did not actually consider herself a transcendentalist, although she dropped such Emersonian comments in her letters as 'I was thinking today – as I noticed, that the "Supernatural", was only the Natural, disclosed'. But she took a more reserved attitude towards God and Nature than Emerson did, although she is very like Thoreau in many ways, as we have seen. Emerson lacked Dickinson's sense of mystery, particularly of the soul as an undiscovered country. She was as much disturbed as reassured by exploring her own psyche, and her view of life is at once more tragic and more comic than Emerson's. Emerson, Calvinism, Shakespeare and the Bible are often said to exhaust the sources with which Dickinson was familiar: but this is an ironically provincial twentieth-century view of nineteenth-century New England college-town intellectual life. Dickinson read Milton, both the Brownings, Ruskin, Keats, Sir Thomas Browne, George Eliot, Quarles, Wordsworth, Shelley, and many other English authors. Sue gave her a copy of Trelawney's *Last Days of Byron and Shelley* in 1859. To what extent should Dickinson be seen in the light of English Romanticism — as well as in the Puritan and transcendental traditions?

Christina Rossetti recognized Dickinson's kinship to the Romantics immediately: 'She had a wonderfully Blakean gift', she wrote when the poems were published posthumously, 'but therewithal a startling recklessness of poetic ways and means'. Some of Dickinson's poems do have a Blakean ring in their pared-down treatment of opposed abstractions. There are echoes of 'The Clod and the Pebble' or 'I was angry with my Friend' in this poem from the 1890 edition which Rossetti read:

> I had no time to Hate –
> Because
> The Grave would hinder Me –
> And Life was not so
> Ample I
> Could finish – Enmity –
>
> Nor had I time to Love –
> But since
> Some Industry must be –
> The little Toil of Love –
> I thought –
> Be large enough for Me –   (478, *c.* 1862)

But the greater similarities are probably with Wordsworth, Keats, and, to a lesser extent, Shelley, in the conviction about the transforming power of the Word.

What is most like Wordsworth in Dickinson is her glorification of childish wisdom, her location of a golden age in early childhood. Sometimes this comes out as a professed anti-intellectualism, despite the reliance on scientific metaphor: 'Arcturus is his other name/I'd rather call him star . . .' (70, *c.* 1859). More typically it emerges as the conviction, expressed in this letter, that children are morally wiser than adults: 'I think the early spiritual influences about a child are more hallowing than we know. The angel begins in the morning in every human life' (c. 1883). Some of Dickinson's poems are pure *Prelude*:

> The Child's faith is new –
> Whole – like his Principle –
> Wide – like the Sunrise
> On fresh Eyes –
> Never had a Doubt –
> Laughs – at a Scruple –
> Believes all sham
> But Paradise –
>
> Credits the World –
> Deems His Dominion
> Broadest of Sovereignties –
> And Caesar – mean –
> In the Comparison –
> Baseless Emperor –
> Ruler of Nought,
> Yet swaying all –
>
> Grown bye and bye
> To hold mistaken
> His pretty estimates
> Of Prickly Things
> He gains the skill
> Sorrowful – as certain –
> Men – to anticipate
> Instead of Kings –   (637, c. 1862)

Wordsworth's infatuation with solitude may also have influenced Dickinson: she marked the passage in the *Excursions* which runs, 'Now to forestall such knowledge as may be/More faithfully collected from himself' (Book II, 'The Solitary'). But this exhortation to rely on a 'columnar Self', as Dickinson phrased it, was common to Puritanism and transcendentalism, too. Dickinson's reclusion comes to look almost inevitable when we realize that everything she read praised seclusion — including *The Imitation of Christ*, another gift from Sue. This is the frustrating part of seeking the literary influences on any author's work. The evidence is generally circumstantial, and we cannot be sure in the reclusion case which source most influenced Dickinson — or whether she came round to solitude in her own independent-minded way, which is just as plausible, if not more so.

The same warning applies to another apparent influence from Wordsworth: the view of the poet as the man who 'rejoices more than other men at the spirit of life that is in him', as the Preface to the *Lyrical Ballads* puts it. In Dickinson the job of poetry is to recapture the transient moment of ecstasy or grief — either emotion, so long as it is profound. Hence her deliberately broken, instantaneous lines, subdivided to a Euclidean point; her startling rhymes; her riddles designed to stun the mind into dropping its defences of humdrum categories. This theme of poetic exhilaration and grandeur is a profound and constant one in Dickinson. During their first meeting she told Higginson, 'If I read a book and it makes my whole body feel so cold no fire can ever warm me, I know that is poetry. If I feel physically as if the top of my head were taken off, I know *that* is poetry. These are the only ways I know it. Is there any other way?'

> To pile like Thunder to its close
> Then crumble grand away
> While Everything created hid
> This – could be Poetry –
>
> Or Love – the two coeval come –
> We both and neither prove –
> Experience either and consume –
> For None see God and live – (1247, *c.* 1873)

The interchangeability of revelation, love and literary beauty is also a Romantic theme, of course, and Dickinson allies truth and beauty in the best Keatsian style:

> I died for Beauty – but was scarce
> Adjusted in the Tomb
> When One who died for Truth, was lain
> In an adjoining Room –

He questioned softly 'Why I failed?'
'For Beauty', I replied –
'And I – for Truth – Themself are One –
We Brethren, are', He said –

And so, as Kinsmen, met a Night –
We talked between the Rooms
Until the Moss had reached our lips –
And covered up our names –   (449, *c.* 1862)

Dickinson is least Calvinist and most Romantic here:

The Definition of Beauty is
That Definition is none –
Of Heaven, easing Analysis,
Since Heaven and He are one.
                        (988, *c.* 1865)

Another similarity to Keats has already been mentioned: negative capability, the Romantic version of the existentialist 'good faith', the ability to tolerate ambiguity and not comfort oneself with the deceptions of dogma. Individuality is a moral burden, rather than a source of enlightenment alone, as it is to the Puritan or to Emerson. We are not allowed to submerge ourselves in creeds or easy beliefs: reality has to remain jagged. Nothing exists for certain except the dissecting mind:

Heaven is so far of the Mind,
That were the Mind dissolved –
The site of it – by Architect
Could not again be proved . . .   (370, *c.* 1862)

There is no saving grace for grief except the purifying intensity of the emotion itself. Like Keats, Dickinson believed that suffering heightened poetic sensitivity and that any intense feeling, good or evil, conferred a sort of moral worth. 'The Anguish of the Avarice/Defrays the Dross of it . . .' (1464). Life is transient and eternity uncertain, but the courage to look on that metaphysical abyss without despair conveys a profound exhilaration:

Go not too near a House of Rose –
The depredation of a Breeze
Or inundation of a Dew
Alarms its walls away –

Nor try to tie the Butterfly,
Nor climb the Bars of Ecstasy,
In insecurity to lie
Is Joy's insuring quality.   (1434, *c*. 1878)

These similarities to the Romantics seem the closest of any we
have traced so far, except perhaps the resemblances to Thoreau.[23]
(Those links are sometimes a little too close for comfort: Mabel
Loomis Todd, Austin's mistress and the poems' editor, was told
ghost stories by Thoreau's mother.) Dickinson has a particularly
impressive amount in common with Keats — down to the odd
coincidence that Keats told a close friend his greatest misfortune
was that he never had a mother, even though his mother was
alive but ailing. But Dickinson was still very much her own
woman — or, if one is determined to be determinist, an inevitably
proud product of the family clannishness. Unlike Blake, she
writes no songs of innocence, it has been said, but only ballads of
disillusioned experience — despite the handicap of having so
little experience to write about. Unlike Wordsworth, she views
nature in the Yankee manner, as a fair but tight-fisted adversary
rather than as a generous benefactress. She takes a far more
aggressive attitude towards the task of wresting meaning from the
thin soil of nature's symbols than either the transcendentalists or
the Romantics. There is a gulf between her own mind and nature,
a mistrust which is largely missing in Wordsworth and Emerson.
Both Keats and Wordsworth take a far more passive, ironically
'feminine' view of the poet's function than Dickinson does. Keats
wrote, 'The Imagination may be compared to Adam's dream —
he awoke and found it true'. In this view, the imagination lies in a
stupor whilst God performs the creative work. To Dickinson the
poet *is* the creator or the surgeon, and her knives are sharper than
any the Romantics used: her wit more incisive, her lines briefer
and more aphoristic, her style more cogent and startlingly modern.

It may be that Keats was able to take a more passive view of poetic creation because he had a muse to help him. Dickinson, being a woman, could not invoke a female muse, and there is no readily available masculine substitute. (Kathleen Raine has spoken of her 'Daimon', whom she sees as a male figure, like Ariel. But she speaks of *consulting* him rather than of purely passive inspiration.)[24] I have suggested that Dickinson was very much her own woman, and the fact that she *was* a woman may mean a great deal. Perhaps all the influences which this chapter has examined must be taken with a grain of salt because of it. We have already seen that Emerson was patronizing about Dickinson's poems and that the Puritan tradition was different for its daughters than for its sons — whether more repressive or more liberating. The same has been said of the Romantic tradition: that Dickinson found it at once exhilarating and forbidding to women. Although there were female novelists before and during the nineteenth century, women poets such as Lydia Sigourney and Felicia Hemans tended to be dismissed as emotional. In any case, the Byronic pose can only be executed in trousers. Elizabeth Barrett Browning wrote, 'Where are the poetesses? I look everywhere for grandmothers and see none'. Although there are resemblances between Dickinson's poems and the Puritan, transcendental, and Romantic traditions, we need to bear in mind that her sex excluded her from full membership in any of these exclusive clubs. It is another good reason for believing her claim that 'I never consciously touch a paint mixed by another person', for avoiding the literary critic's equivalent of the stereotypes dismissed in chapter 1 — that is, the view that Dickinson was either Jonathan Edwards, Emerson, or Wordsworth in petticoats. (If she was to be called anything in petticoats, she would probably have preferred to be labelled a hyena, as Wollstonecraft was.) The determinist view is patronizing, of course, just as the myths tend to be, because it risks portraying Dickinson as derivative, and playing down the extent of her professionalism and creativity. She is far too enigmatic for over-simplification, and none of the influences wholly explains her. In part this is because she may consciously have set out to make both her life and work a riddle.

Notes

1. Edwin Arlington Robinson, 'New England', in Louis Untermeyer (ed.), *Modern American and Modern British Poetry* (New York: Harcourt, Brace and World, 1955), p.41.
2. Jay Martin, *Harvests of Change: American Literature 1865–1914* (Englewood Cliffs, NJ: Prentice-Hall, 1967), p.145.
3. Ibid., p. 150.
4. Ibid., p. 151.
5. Sewall, *Life*, vol. 1, p. 26.
6. William Whately, *A Bride-Bush, or, A Direction for Married Persons* (London, 1619), quoted in Karl Keller, *The Only Kangaroo among the Beauty* (Baltimore and London: Johns Hopkins Press, 1979), p. 12.
7. Elsa Green, 'Emily Dickinson was a Poetess', *College English* 34 (1972), quoted in Keller, *Kangaroo*, p.11, fn.
8. George Herbert, 'Prayer', in Helen Gardner (ed.), *The New Oxford Book of English Verse 1250–1950* (London: Book Club Associates, 1975), p. 255.
9. Ralph Waldo Emerson, third and fourth stanzas of 'Good-Bye', from *Poems* (London: A.P. Watt and Sons, 1904).
10. Emerson, quoted in Keller, *Kangaroo*.
11. Emerson in a letter of 1858, quoted in Keller, *Kangaroo*, p. 158.
12. Clark Griffith, *The Long Shadow: Emily Dickinson's Tragic Poetry* (Princeton UP, 1964), p. 268.
13. Henry David Thoreau, 'An Essay on Civil Disobedience', in Carl Bode (ed.), *The Portable Thoreau* (New York: Viking paperback, 1947), p. 121.
14. Thoreau, *Walden*, in *The Portable Thoreau*, pp. 382–3.
15. Griffith, *Shadow*.
16. Quoted in Edward Wagenknecht, *Henry David Thoreau: What Manner of Man?* (Amherst: University of Massachusetts Press, 1981), p. 26.
17. Sewall, *Life*, vol. 1, p. 21.
18. For these and other Vermonter jokes, see Raymond Smullyam, *What Is the Name of this Book?* (Harmondsworth: Pelican Books, 1981).
19. The term used by George F. Whicher in his chapter on Dickinson's humour (from *This Was a Poet*, New York: Scribner's, 1938, repr. in Richard B. Sewall, ed., *Emily Dickinson: A Collection of Critical Essays*, Englewood Cliffs, NJ: Prentice-Hall, 1963, pp. 41–4).
20. Robert Frost, 'Provide, Provide', in Untermeyer (ed.), *Modern Poetry*, p. 81.
21. Whicher, in Sewall, *Essays*, p. 41.
22. Gelpi, *Mind*, p. 91.
23. Joanne Diehl argues this case cogently in *Dickinson and the Romantic Imagination* (Princeton UP, 1981).
24. Interview in Robin Skelton, *The Practice of Poetry* (London: Heinemann, 1975), pp. 27–8.

3 Riddle

Tell all the Truth but tell it slant –
Success in Circuit lies
Too bright for our infirm Delight
The Truth's superb surprise

As Lightning to the Children eased
With explanation kind
The Truth must dazzle gradually
Or every man be blind –   (1129, *c.* 1868)

Candor – my tepid Friend –
Come not to play with me . . .   (1537, *c.* 1881)

Riddle recurs constantly in Dickinson's work and biography. Her life appears a paradox: to reverse Robinson's poem, she, the New Englander, cries wildest who has drunk the least. The paucity of events in her life belies the breadth of the enormous poetic output — nearly 1,800 poems, about 350 attributed by handwriting to one year alone, 1862. The love poems have no known object: as the first chapter showed, this conundrum has generated puzzlement, literary gossip galore, and some very grandiose claims. Dickinson's self-enforced seclusion is another riddle, and, like the one posed by the sphinx at the crossroads, it has felled many travellers through her verse. Was her reclusion a sign of eccentricity — even lunacy — or a deliberate confronting of only the essential in life? And is the enigmatic, spare style she adopted in her writing an indication of incompetence or of professional skill? I shall examine the riddle of Dickinson's life, as embodied in her reclusion, in chapter 4. This chapter will be concerned with riddle in the poems. But there is a link between the life and the poems: it has been said that riddle was so central to Dickinson's work that she made her life into a deliberate conundrum.[1]

Riddle is an ancient device in English poetry, with roots in Saxon literature and folk verse.[2] Probably one of the best-known examples of riddle in ballad is 'I gave my love a cherry':

I gave my love a cherry that had no stone.
I gave my love a chicken that had no bone.
I gave my love a ring that had no end.
I gave my love a baby with no crying.

How can there be a cherry that has no stone?
How can there be a chicken that has no bone?
How can there be a ring that has no end?
How can there be a baby with no crying?

A cherry when it's blooming, it has no stone.
A chicken in the egg, it has no bone.
A ring when it's rolling, it has no end.
A baby when it's sleeping, there's no crying.

Nursery rhyme is another source of riddle in verse: 'How many miles to Babylon?' and 'As I was going to St Ives' are well-known examples. There are others:

The man in the wilderness asked of me,
'How many strawberries grow in the sea?'
I answered him as I thought good,
'As many red herrings as grow in the wood'.

Humpty Dumpty lies in the beck,
With a white counterpane round his neck.
Forty doctors and forty wrights
Cannot put Humpty Dumpty to rights.   (On an egg)

Flour of England, fruit of Spain
Met together in a shower of rain,
Put in a bag tied round with a string.
If you tell me this riddle, I'll give you a ring.
                                    (On plum-pudding)

Every lady in this land
Has twenty nails on each hand
Five and twenty hands and feet.
All this is true, without deceit.
                          (Watch the punctuation!)

The use of riddle may be as much an indication of nursery rhyme's influence on Dickinson as is her style of short quatrains and frequent personification, also seen in such children's rhymes as 'Don't care was made to care'.

But the importance of nursery rhyme for Dickinson can be over-emphasized: we have already seen that she was a well-read and scientifically educated woman, not a childlike primitive. There are other reasons why she uses riddle so often. The laconic mode of speech she adopts, a reflection of the New England taciturnity, stands out very effectively in riddle, as it does in aphorism. Yankees are known for answering a question with another question. Sometimes Dickinson seems not to be able to help herself, to use a riddling style of speech compulsively.

> Safe in their Alabaster Chambers –
> Untouched by Morning –
> And untouched by Noon –
> Lie the meek members of the Resurrection –
> Rafter of Satin – and Roof of Stone!
>
> Grand go the Years – in their Crescent – above them –
> Worlds scoop their Arcs –
> And Firmaments – row –
> Diadems – drop – and Doges – surrender –
> Soundless as dots – on a Disc of Snow –
>
> (216, version of 1861)

The third line of the second stanza puzzles through its tightness with words. 'Arrange themselves in a row', it must mean: 'row' in the sense of 'argue' does not exist in American parlance, and the other possibility for a verb, rowing a boat, makes no sense. It has been said that Dickinson's use of riddle is inadvertent. a sign of poor craftsmanship. The fact that her lines are sometimes obscure is put down to her amateurish inability to see beyond the confines of hymn measure. When she cannot pare a thought to the required number of syllables, this argument runs, she sacrifices the thought's clarity. She does not choose to set her thought in riddles: she has riddle thrust upon her through her poetic incompetence.[3]

I think this argument is generally mistaken, even if it is a

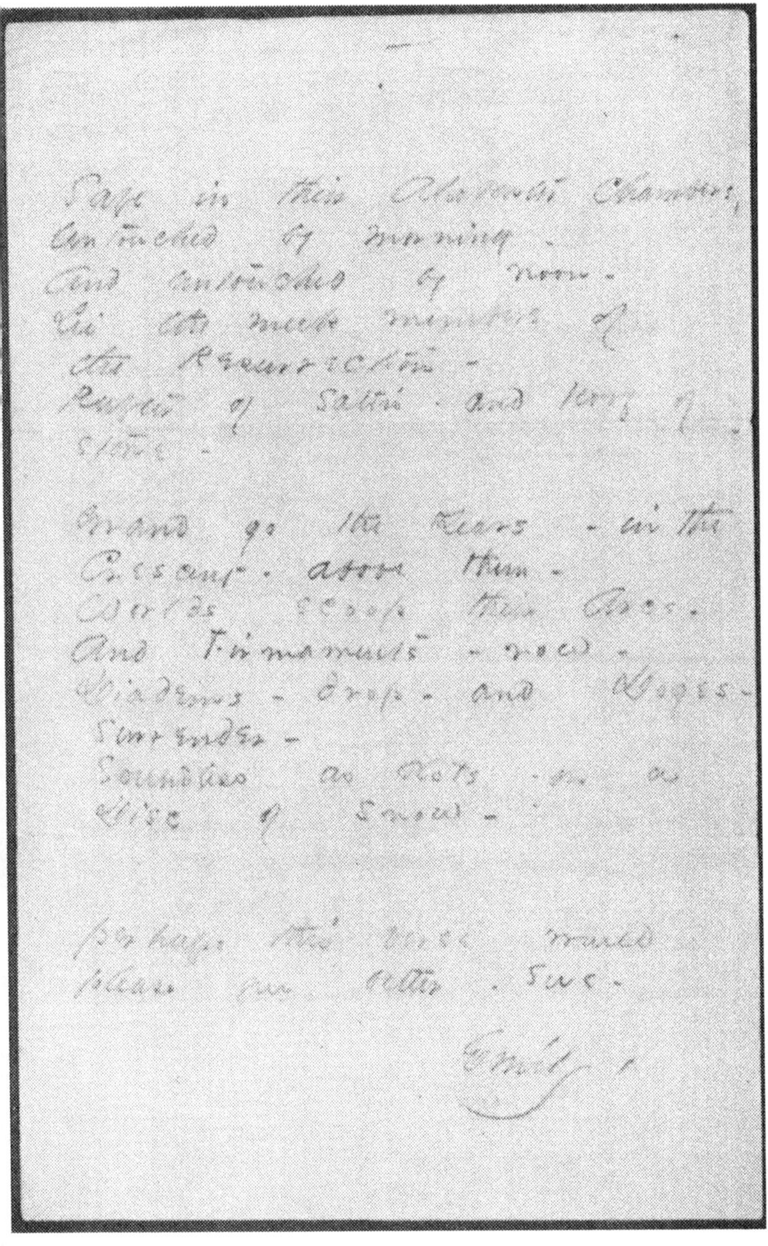

'Safe in their Alabaster Chambers' (*see facing page*)

Edward Dickinson by O. A. Bullard, 1840

Emily Norcross Dickinson by O. A. Bullard, 1840

(*above*) The Homestead on Main Street, Amherst
(*left*) Edward Dickinson, dated variously 1853, 1860, 1874

Susan Gilbert Dickinson, *ca* 1851

Samuel Bowles

refreshing departure from the modern trend of Dickinson hagiolatry. Although reading Dickinson requires concentration, and a willingness to fill in some blanks, her meanings are generally clear enough.[4] Some of the riddle poems are quite straightforward:

> I like to see it lap the Miles –
> And lick the Valleys up –
> And stop to feed itself at Tanks –
> And then – prodigious step
>
> Around a Pile of Mountains –
> And supercilious peer
> In Shanties – by the sides of Roads –
> And then a Quarry pare
>
> To fit its Ribs
> And crawl between
> Complaining all the while
> In horrid – hooting stanza –
> Then chase itself down Hill –
>
> And neigh like Boanerges –
> Then – punctual as a Star
> Stop – docile and omnipotent –
> At its own stable door –   (585, *c.* 1862)
>
> A Visitor in Marl –
> Who influences Flowers –
> Till they are orderly as Busts –
> And Elegant – as Glass –
>
> Who visits in the Night –
> And just before the Sun –
> Concludes his glistening interview –
> Caresses – and is gone –
>
> But whom his fingers touched –
> And where his feet have run –
> And whatsoever Mouth he kissed –
> Is as it had not been –   (391, *c.* 1862)

57

A narrow Fellow in the Grass
Occasionally rides –
You may have met Him – did you not?
His notice sudden is –

The Grass divides as with a Comb
A spotted shaft is seen –
And then it closes at your feet
And opens further on –

He likes a boggy Acre
A Floor too cool for Corn –
Yet when a Boy, and barefoot –
I more than once at Noon

Have passed, I thought, a Whip lash
Unbraiding in the Sun
When stooping to secure it
It wrinkled, and was gone –

Several of Nature's People
I know, and they know me –
I feel for them a transport
Of cordiality –

But never met this Fellow
Attended, or alone
Without a tighter breathing
And Zero at the Bone –   (986, *c.* 1864)

Nor is Dickinson enslaved by the Common Measure of hymn
metre, the alternating four- and three-beat lines. Tetrameters *are*
her commonest choice — and they are a bold risk in English,
whose natural rhythm is iambic pentameter. John Crowe Ransom, who introduced the claim that Dickinson learnt her metres
from 'her father's hymnbook', makes the dogmatic assertion that
pentameter is the only meter for complex thought. Aside from
being intolerant and narrow, this is ironic: Dickinson has also
been chastised for letting the choice of metre come first, as we saw
earlier, but this is what Ransom seems to advocate. Accepting

Ransom's view would lead one to the outside-in conclusion that because Dickinson rarely wrote in pentameter, few of her thoughts can be very complex. In any case, she experimented successfully with other metres and rhyme schemes, such as this one, which she could not have found in 'her father's hymnbook':

> A Spider sewed at Night
> Without a Light
> Upon an Arc of White.
>
> If Ruff it was of Dame
> Or Shroud of Gnome
> Himself himself inform.
>
> Of Immortality
> His Strategy
> Was Physiognomy.   (1138, *c*. 1869)

I do not accept that Dickinson was forced to use riddle because she lacked professional skill. Even in the atypically obscure case of 'Safe in their Alabaster Chambers', the confusing line 'Firmaments – row' — whether or not devised by the outside-in procedure of sacrificing meaning to rigid form — is preferable to the trite original second stanza.

> Light laughs the breeze
> In her Castle above them –
> Babbles the Bee in a stolid Ear,
> Pipe the Sweet Birds in ignorant cadence –
> Ah, what sagacity perished here!
>   (216, version of 1859)

The extent to which she revised this poem — with Sue's help — itself reflects professionalism, particularly because the original version had been good enough for the *Springfield Republican* to publish anonymously in 1861.

To argue that riddle is the outcome of Dickinson's sacrifice of content to form is also mistaken, I think, because most practising writers deny that there is any distinction between style and meaning. Orwell, for example, thought that careful expression both enhanced and reflected painstaking thought — a two-way relationship. Dickinson used riddle *consciously* because it was a form which embodied the content central to her work — paradox, secrecy and play. It was always immediacy she was after, and riddle *is* paradoxical, secretive, playful: it does not merely talk about these qualities at second hand. Riddle startles us into listening, as does aphorism: both surprise us into 'trust in the Unexpected' (555). Emersonian grandeur, on the other hand, flows over the mind in a Lethe-like ooze. Riddle makes us work to understand, and that, to a descendant of the Puritans, is valuable in itself. In any case, it is the only means of grasping the things worth having:

> The Spirit is the Conscious Ear.
> We actually Hear
> When We inspect – that's audible –
> That is admitted – Here –
>
> For other Services – as Sound –
> There hangs a smaller Ear
> Outside the Castle – that Contain –
> The other – only Hear –   (733, *c.* 1863)

It is this power to goad the mind that Dickinson values in riddle and paradox. Even in the poems which are not specifically couched as riddles, she uses a Metaphysical's quantity of paradox, although only in this one poem does she explicitly label it so:

> Experience is the Angled Road
> Preferred against the Mind
> By – Paradox – the Mind itself –
> Presuming it to lead
>
> Quite opposite – How Complicate
> The Discipline of Man –
> Compelling Him to choose Himself
> His Preappointed Pain –   (901, *c.* 1864)

This is an entirely typical poem: the half-rhymes, the abstraction, the Latinate words balanced against the Lutheran hymn rhythms, the envoy of the word 'pain'. But perhaps the paradoxical juxtaposition of seeming opposites, practical experience and abstract thought, is particularly typical. 'Opposite' is highlighted by its position at the start of the second stanza and strengthened by the elision of the sense from the first stanza — a feature common in Dickinson, by the way, but beyond the reach of most hymn writers. Sometimes Dickinson fashions her paradoxes and riddles into almost Donne-like conceits:

> Me from Myself – to banish –
> Had I Art –
> Impregnable my Fortress
> Unto All Heart –
>
> But since Myself – assault Me –
> How have I peace
> Except by subjugating
> Consciousness?
>
> And since We're mutual Monarch
> How this be
> Except by Abdication –
> Me – of Me?   (642, *c.* 1862)

Here again Dickinson leaves out a necessary word, in the second line of the last stanza — no doubt for the sake of the rhythm, although the problem might be solved by replacing 'how' with 'can'. But the meaning is still clear, and the rest of the poem can hardly be accused of roughness or professional incompetence. Nor does it manifest the philosophical naïvety which stereotype sometimes attributes to Dickinson. The question of consciousness's own awareness of itself still occupies modern philosophy of mind. Dickinson has used paradox, and the riddle of the second stanza, to ask a perennial philosophical question in the neatest poetic form.

Sometimes Dickinson's use of paradox does threaten rather than enhance her poetry. Paradox comes a little too easily to her: it is not always as startling as she intends it to be, and sometimes it is even clichéd:

> It might be lonelier
> Without the Loneliness –
> I'm so accustomed to my Fate – . . .
>> (405, *c.* 1862)

> Death – unto itself – Exception –
> Is exempt from Change – . . .   (749, *c.* 1863)

But in general, paradox enables Dickinson to present her unique and troubled awareness that although we have no choice but to be self-sufficient, we can never have sufficient knowledge of our own motives. We are perverse riddles to ourselves:

> I had a daily Bliss
> I half indifferent viewed
> Till sudden I perceived it stir –
> It grew as I pursued
>
> Till when around a Height
> It wasted from my sight
> Increased beyond my utmost scope
> I learned to estimate.   (1057, *c.* 1865)

In this poem we never learn what the 'Bliss' was, only that it is gone. The joy's content is itself a riddle, and such uncertainty also lends power to this mighty poem about pain:

> After great pain, a formal feeling comes –
> The Nerves sit ceremonious, like Tombs –
> The stiff Heart questions, was it He, that bore,
> And yesterday, or Centuries before?
>
> The Feet, mechanical, go round –
> Of Ground, or Air, or Ought –
> A Wooden way
> Regardless grown,
> A Quartz contentment, like a stone –

This is the hour of Lead –
Remembered, if outlived,
As Freezing persons, recollect the Snow –
First – Chill – then Stupor – then the letting go –
(341, *c.* 1862)

This is a poem which startles in every respect, treating a grandiose subject scrupulously without cliché. It switches metres, beginning with pentameter — had Ransom not read this well-known work? – and moving on to tetrameter and trimeter. It juxtaposes rhymes dangerously — 'round' and 'ground' in the second stanza. It personifies the verb 'ought' into a noun. It borrows an archaic use of 'and' ('only') in the fourth line of the first stanza. But the real puzzle, the great riddle which the reader most wants to solve, is what the pain was. This Dickinson never reveals: she 'forestalls the dishonor', as she said in the letter to Higginson which explains why she had no portrait taken after her college days. It is no wonder that speculation has flourished. The riddle of the life is never very far away from the riddle of the poems, but it is still a mistake to become too much diverted by it. The poem would be very much less powerful, less universal, if we knew that the pain was rejection by burly Samuel Bowles, Kate Scott Anthon's heterosexuality, being an old maid, or even my favourite candidate, failure to publish. Dickinson knew how to keep her secrets, and we must be content to keep them too. In examining the relation between Dickinson's life and work, we must be content with negative capability.

Dickinson kept her answers secret on purpose:

The Riddle we can guess
We speedily despise –
Not anything is stale so long
As Yesterday's surprise – (1222, *c.* 1870)

Her reclusion, to be examined further in the next chapter, is consistent with her use of riddle and secrecy: the poetry that relies on these devices is itself reclusive. Its themes are the great secrets:

Absence disembodies – so does Death
Hiding individuals from the Earth

> Superstition helps, as well as love –
> Tenderness decreases as we prove –
>
>   (860, *c.* 1864)

This single quatrain overflows with paradox and riddle. Although we bury the dead, 'Death' hides us from the 'Earth': how can this be? It seems as apparently nonsensical a statement as the paradox offered by another New Englander, Wallace Stevens, in 'Peter Quince at the Clavier': 'Beauty is momentary in the mind/The fitful tracing of a portal;/But in the flesh it is immortal'.[5] If I had to play Oedipus to Dickinson's sphinx, I would suggest that the first pair of lines is about love: absence and death heighten our feeling for the loved one — taken for granted when alive, perhaps. Memory hides the beloved from fleshly mortality. This interpretation seems consistent with the second couplet, which introduces superstition 'as well as love' — love being the subject already treated. Here again, by 'superstition' Dickinson means 'negative capability', the deliberate keeping of secrets — an odd anti-intellectualism for a writer who uses natural scientific metaphor so generously. The more we investigate things rationally, the drier and less capable of love our natures become: 'tenderness decreases as we prove'. What we can prove is, in any case, limited: Dickinson almost anticipates Heisenberg's uncertainty principle.

> Perception of an Object costs
> Precise the Object's loss –
> Perception is itself a Gain
> Replying to its Price.   (1071, *c.* 1866)

The worth of the riddle is in the guessing, not in the answer.

Riddle enables Dickinson to take on the grand themes without mawkishness: it lets her play with them. Play is central to poetry, but playing with ideas as a child plays — seriously. Dickinson's work is attractive because it is never anything but serious about the cosmic riddles, although it expects few answers. If we insist on answers to the great mysteries, we lose what chance we have of solving them: the ultimate paradox in her thought. We must remain open to the several possible solutions — and possibility is poetry's domain.

I dwell in Possibility
A fairer House than Prose –
More numerous of Windows –
Superior – for Doors –

Of Chambers as the Cedars –
Impregnable of Eye –
And for an Everlasting Roof
The Gambrels of the Sky –

Of Visitors – the fairest –
For Occupation – This –
The spreading wide my narrow Hands
To gather Paradise –   (657, *c.* 1862)

Riddle, games, imagination and poetry are joyful and liberating, our only remaining links with the child's superior comprehension. Prose is for the captive adult mind:

They shut me up in Prose –
As when a little Girl
They put me in the Closet –
Because they liked me 'still' –

Still! Could themself have peeped –
And seen my Brain – go round –
They might as wise have lodged a Bird
For Treason – in the Pound –

Himself has but to will
And easy as a Star
Abolish his Captivity
And laugh – No more have I –   (613, *c.* 1862)

We have already seen that Dickinson viewed riddle as a means for heightening awareness, and that she viewed this higher consciousness as a goal in itself. Perhaps this is too dry a way of putting it. Riddles serve all these functions in Dickinson's work, but they are also fun — and Dickinson's poems are full of fun, despite the dour stereotype. She uses the word 'joy' without

embarrassment, even though gloom is more everyday poetic fare
— just as the symptoms for painfulness outweigh those for
pleasurableness by two to one in Roget's thesaurus.

> In many and reportless places
> We feel a Joy –
> Reportless also, but sincere as Nature
> Or Deity –
>
> It comes without a consternation –
> Dissolves – the same –
> But leaves a sumptuous Destitution –
> Without a Name –
>
> Profane it by a search – we cannot
> It has no home –
> Nor we who having once inhaled it –
> Thereafter roam.   (1382, *c.* 1876)

Sheer joy glints off even this late-life riddle about the wind, like
light off a metallic whirligig:

> A Route of Evanescence
> With a revolving Wheel –
> A Resonance of Emerald –
> A Rush of Cochineal –
> And every Blossom on the Bush
> Adjusts its tumbled Head –
> The mail from Tunis, probably,
> An easy Morning's Ride –   (1463, *c.* 1879)

Wind enjoyed a special status in transcendentalist symbolism:
it was the breath of the spirit. Thoreau said that 'In enthusiasm
we undulate to the divine spiritus — as the lake to the wind'.
Wind is a frequent emblem for exhilaration in Dickinson, too:

> Exhilaration is the Breeze
> That lifts us from the Ground
> And leaves us in another place
> Where statement is not found.
>
>   (1118, *c.* 1868)

If 'statement is not found' in the country where exhilaration conveys us, its inhabitants must speak in nothing but riddles.

Dickinson's use of riddle in her poetry is of a piece with her emphasis on playful exhilaration, her love of secrecy, and her fascination with paradox. Perhaps it is a conscious revolt against the wizened late-Puritan thought — or the simplistic revivalism — which held that all the cosmic mysteries had received their official answer.[6] Or perhaps Dickinson uses riddle because she is nevertheless deeply and unconsciously Puritan: because to the Calvinist the profound, unanswerable riddle is whether she will be granted God's grace. In any case, Dickinson's use of riddle is a deliberate and skilful technique which helped her to avoid the pathos and bathos which dominated the poetry of her day. But if her reliance on riddle was conscious in her poetry, was it equally conscious in her life? Did she in fact set out to make her life a metaphor for her poetry? It is now time to turn to the riddle of reclusion in Dickinson's life, and to its reflection in her poems about silence and solitude.

Notes

1. This is the view Sewall takes in his biography. It seems a bit too calculating to me, but it does at least credit Dickinson with will and determination, rather than seeing her as a pitiable recluse. And it gives the professional primacy over the personal: the personal was fashioned to suit the professional aim.
2. For the use of riddle in Dickinson's poetry, see Dolores Dyer Lucas, *Emily Dickinson and Riddle* (Dekalb, Ill.: Northern Ill. Press, 1969). For examples of riddle in Anglo-Saxon literature, see Kevin Crossley-Holland, *The Riddle Book* (London, 1982).
3. This is the view taken by David Porter in *Dickinson: The Modern Idiom* (Cambridge, Mass.: Harvard UP, 1981).
4. Emily Stipes Watts agrees with this evaluation in her chapter on Dickinson in *The Poetry of American Women from 1632 to 1945* (Austin and London: University of Texas Press, 1977).
5. Wallace Stevens, 'Peter Quince at the Clavier', in Untermeyer (ed.), *Modern Poetry*, p. 100.
6. Sewall suggests this idea in his biography.

4 Reclusion

'Half-cracked' to Higginson, living,
afterward famous in garbled versions,
your hoard of dazzling scraps a battlefield,
now your old snood

mothballed at Harvard
and you in your variorum monument
equivocal to the end —
who are you?

Gardening the day-lily,
wiping the wine-glass stems,
your thought pulsed on behind
a forehead battered paper-thin,

you, woman, masculine
in single-mindedness,
for whom the word was more
than a symptom —

a condition of being.
Till the air buzzing with spoiled language
sang in your ears
of Perjury

and in your half-cracked way you chose
silence for entertainment,
chose to have it out at last
on your own premises.'[1]

Was Dickinson's withdrawal from the world proof that she was
half or even wholly 'cracked'? Or was it her way of ensuring time
to write and to experience poetic exhilaration? Another woman
writer, Eudora Welty, has recently written that she was always
aware she 'needed more Vail' [sic], as Dickinson once wrote in a

letter. 'My temperament and my instinct had told me alike that the author, who writes at his own emergency, remains and needs to remain at his private remove. I wished to be, not effaced, but invisible — actually a powerful position.'[2] Was Dickinson a pitiable hermit or a determined and diligent acolyte of the muse? Did she choose reclusion, or was it thrust upon her?

Before we begin to answer these questions, we must evaluate how complete and how important Dickinson's reclusion was. It is the centre of the myth, harped upon in endless stories of Dickinson talking to her few visitors from behind half-closed doors or the top of the stairs. She is said to have emerged from her room only once a year, when she underwent a Cinderella-like transmogrification into the brilliant hostess of her father's annual college reception. Supposedly she lowered sweetmeats to village children down a string dangling from her first-floor bedroom window. Not only is the reclusion portrayed as near-total in the myth: it is seen as the only important facet of her character, as an all-absorbing obsession to Dickinson herself and as the most interesting aspect of her life and work to biographers and readers.

But the poet and her family refused to rise to this bait. Reclusion is a less common theme in the poems than religion, which will be considered in the next chapter. Her sister Vinnie described Emily's seclusion as 'only a happen', brought on by the demands of an invalid mother and a twelve-room house with few servants. As I have mentioned above, neither Austin nor Vinnie saw anything startling in Emily's staying at home. Dickinson kept up her letter-writing throughout her life, read widely and retentively, and retained an interest in current events — even if her preferred form of news, in the best mortuary merriment manner, seems to have been accounts of fatal accidents. When Bowles shouted at her to come down and talk to him, she did so with perfect aplomb and no sign of irrationality: perhaps she could put on the eccentric manner and take it off again. Or perhaps there was nothing eccentric about it in her eyes. Sewall claims that Dickinson deliberately turned her life into a riddle, a metaphor, a vehicle of her work — that she was in full control of herself even in her apparent outlandishness. He prefers to treat Dickinson's reclusion as a conscious, rational, emblematic choice. It is more productive and less patronizing to see her that way than as the agoraphobic lunatic of flashing and inexplicable genius.

But although the usual myths about Dickinson's reclusion can probably be dismissed, there are still grounds for doubting that she chose obscurity — particularly poetic obscurity, as I shall discuss further in chapter 6. In her later years Dickinson seems to have regretted her inability to meet her friends face to face. The letters contain apologies such as this one, written in 1883: 'I had hoped to see you, but have no grace to talk, and my own words so chill and burn me, that the temperature of other Minds is too new an Awe'. In 1884 she wrote this apology to other friends whom she had refused to see: 'In all the circumference of Expression, those guileless words of Adam and Eve never were surpassed, "I was afraid and hid myself"'. Some of her later poems demonstrate very little pleasure in seclusion, such as this 1877 one which is addressed to Kate Scott Anthon, in seeming confirmation of the lesbian thesis.

> I shall not murmur if at last
> The ones I loved below
> Permission have to understand
> For what I shunned them so –
> Divulging it would rest my Heart
> But it would ravage theirs –
> Why, Katie, Treason has a voice –
> But mine – dispels – in Tears.
>
> (1410, *c.* 1877)

The chiaroscuro of her early tone, the quick flitting from somberness to glinting joy, deepened into somewhat more shadow as she aged. If reclusion was a deliberate, Thoreauvian confronting of the essential in life when she was thirty, it may have become a compulsive habit by her forties and fifties. And even when she was young, there was a fear of freedom about her:

> A Prison gets to be a Friend –
> Between its Ponderous face
> And Ours – a Kinsmanship express –
> And in its narrow Eyes –
>
> We come to look with gratitude
> For the appointed Beam

It deal us – stated as our food –
And hungered for – the same . . .

The narrow Round – the Stint –
The slow exchange of Hope –
For something passiver – Content –
Too steep for looking up –

The Liberty we knew
Avoided – like a Dream –
Too wide for any Night but Heaven –
If That – indeed – redeem   (652, *c*. 1862)

Why would Dickinson deliberately choose reclusion? The practical grounds were impeccable: 'If people were held off, they
could not make the myriad and constant demands of time and
service which the Victorian spinster was expected to render
without hesitation'.[3] The mid-nineteenth century was an
outward-looking time in New England. Its female epitomes were
abolitionists like Harriet Beecher Stowe, proponents of women's
rights and the Italian nationalist cause like Margaret Fuller,
self-supporting novelists who travelled the frontier like Helen
Hunt Jackson. Jackson was an Amherst girl, and throughout her
life Dickinson was exposed to women of this active ilk. Her
botany book, which held that 'The study of Botany naturally
leads the mind to greater love and reverence for the Deity', was
written by an enormously popular female educator, Almira Lin-
coln Phelps of Troy Female Seminary. The president of Mount
Holyoke, Mary Lyon, was cast in the same empirical and
evangelical mould. Many of Dickinson's class-mates led lives of a
remarkable fullness, balancing marriage and child-rearing with
missionary work, lecturing, social work, or literary success.

High standards were set for an educated and intelligent New
England woman in Dickinson's time. Even one of lesser ability
was expected to make duty calls, help the sick and impoverished,
do the church's bidding, care for aged relatives, serve on com-
mittees, and demonstrate other equivalents of the masculine civic-
mindedness which led Samuel Fowler Dickinson to bankrupt
himself in providing his native town with its college. Dickinson
had no taste for these pursuits: as we have seen, she was remark-

ably unencumbered with charity or civic concern. Whilst her class-mates journeyed the world in good causes, she stayed in the family home and saw her name in print only once, when she won second prize for rye and Indian bread at the Amherst show. She rejected suggestions that she should embark on good works after she left Mount Holyoke:

> The halt – the lame – and the blind – the old – the infirm – the bed-ridden – the super-annuated – the ugly, and disagreeable – the perfectly hateful to me – all *these* to see, and be seen by – an opportunity rare for cultivating meekness – and patience – and submission – and for turning my back to this very sinful and wicked world. Somehow or other I incline to other things.

It is striking how rarely her poems of the years 1861–5 mention the Civil War: their preoccupation with other concerns some-times seems like the equivalent of Austin's buying a substitute for the draft. As her friends married and left for their active lives, as the invitations to the taffy-pulls and skating parties dwindled, Dickinson turned inward partly through choice, partly through disregard of her expected altruistic role, and partly through lack of anything else to do. She could not compete with her old friends in any way but through her poetry, and poetry was held in some distrust by her educators, who branded Shakespeare's sonnets libertine. Perhaps Dickinson was making the best of a bad thing — her inability to emulate her 'useful' women friends — by turning inward to write poetry. At least she could work at it with the requisite high-mindedness and discipline — so long as she could maintain her solitude. Dedication it clearly required: no one writes 350 poems in one year during the odd afternoons when the weather is too inclement for charity calls on Irish railway workers' shanties.

But although Dickinson's reclusion kept the outside world at bay, it never freed her altogether for her poetry — which makes the extent of her output all the more remarkable. The 'Queen Recluse' (as Bowles called her) is often portrayed as a child in her father's home, with a twentieth-century child's lack of responsi-bilities. Even some modern feminist criticism sees her this way: 'Practically speaking, remaining a daughter may have been the only way to keep herself free from responsibilities so that she could write poetry', and, even more strongly, 'The themes and attitudes expressed in Emily Dickinson's poems are not informed by her adult experience'.[4] But this claim ignores the extensive duties of the nineteenth-century daughter-at-home. The Victorian period may have held that women had a natural and childlike faith — an expectation which seems to have tormented Dickinson, who did not — but, like most centuries before our own child-centred one, it rarely allowed its daughters to be childlike in other ways, even in girlhood. From their adolescence American daughters were exhorted to keep diaries of their moral development — the good Puritan's balance sheet with God. They were told they must strive for spiritual perfection, not only for the sake of their own salvation, but for the good of their brothers, fathers, and beaux, whose contact with the sharp business world and high natural passions excused them from similar strictness with themselves. Dickinson seems to have taken these duties on as expected: as I mentioned in chapter 1, she believed that it was her duty to make everything pleasant at home for her father and brother. In practical matters, the daughter-at-home's duties were no less all-encompassing. Dickinson is generally pictured as dusting the odd vase, or polishing the wine-glass stem, before nipping upstairs to dash off a quick masterpiece. In fact we know that the women of the Dickinson household did much heavy work: Vinnie double-dug the garden. Exactly how the sisters worked out the division of labour is somewhat unclear, but, at a minimum, Emily had to care for her mother (who was ill from the mid-1850s), prepare a good deal of the food, and perform some housework and gardening. These duties came before writing, even for published and acknowledged 'women of genius', which she was not. 'Every literary lady was at pains to point out that she never lifted a pen until the last dish was done.'[5] Even Lydia Huntley Sigourney, the first American poet of either sex to make a living from her pen, had this acerbic comment to make:

> . . . Here's a littering shred
> Of linen left behind — a vile reproach
> To all good housewifery. Right glad am I
> That no neat lady, trained in ancient times
> Of pudding-making, and of sampler work,

And speckless sanctity of household care,
Hath happened here to spy thee. She, no doubt,
Keen looking through her spectacles, would say,
"This comes of reading books": or some spruce beau,
Essenc'd and lily-handed, had he chanc'd
To scan thy slight superfices, 'twould be
"This comes of writing poetry".[6]

The deliberate choice of reclusion could not completely liberate Dickinson from household duties. In any case, husbanding carefully what time remained for writing might have been rational enough, but taking time off for visitors and then requiring them to talk from behind a half-closed door was another — if that story is true. Even if Dickinson's seclusion was based on practical grounds which the myths ignore, and even if stereotype has exaggerated its extent and romanticized its causes, the withdrawal was still more extreme than the demands of her craft required. Indeed, it may have harmed her craft, narrowing her field of reference. Certainly it tempted her into short-cuts of speech which only she could understand: she uses "the Tyrian" to mean 'light' in one poem (152), an elision which is only understandable to someone who has read a previous poem (140) in which she mentions Tyrian-blue light. If Dickinson's reclusion was neither a perfectly rational choice nor a sure proof of lunacy, what does explain it?

One explanation which has been suggested recently is that Dickinson made a *rational*, Hamlet-like decision to *appear* mad. This antic disposition — and remember that Austin said his sister was good at posing — was not simply a means of holding the outside world at bay to make time for writing, but a careful alteration of the Byronic poet's cloak to fit Dickinson's petite female form. Dickinson deliberately chose a role to play, in order to overcome the double bind which women poets are said to face: women are not meant to be assertive and self-absorbed, but poets have to be. It was as deliberate a pose as Whitman's self-congratulatory expansiveness or Hemingway's machismo, but it was a different sort of pose because she was a woman. She chose a Gothic persona because that was the only one manufactured in women's sizes. 'By literally and figuratively impersonating "a woman-white", Dickinson wove her life into a gothic "yarn of pearl" that gave her exactly the "Amplitude" and "Awe" she knew she needed in order to write great poetry.[7] The personal was put in bondage to the professional — to such an extent that Dickinson eventually 'halfcracked' under the strain. In the end Dickinson was both a deliberate impersonation of a lunatic and a genuine madwoman.

This argument appears to reconcile the traditional stereotype of 'poor mad Emily' with the more typically modern picture of 'a tough-minded independent woman whose self-doubt and timidities were a mask'.[8] It is not a completely unorthodox marriage: Martha Dickinson Bianchi, who was responsible in large part for the jilting myth, also said that her aunt once pretended to lock the door of the bedroom when she was visiting, turned to her, and remarked, 'Mattie: here's freedom'. Nor is it a combination of seeming opposites which would have been out of character for Emily, with her Dickinson hauteur, her shrewdness, her posing, and her ability to manipulate the other members of the family to her advantage. She often seems to have had the upper hand of her father, despite the tyrant stereotype. She persuaded Vinnie to do most of the errands — at least according to Vinnie. If her disparaging comments to Higginson are any indication, she seems to have lorded it over her mother. And the 'smallest room' in which she claimed to have immured herself was actually the best bedroom in the Homestead.

Where the 'deliberate madness' view does tread on thin ice, however, is in its assertion that a female poet can only solve the double bind by choosing to become 'the madwoman in the attic'. Perhaps one would not need to make this claim in order to explain Dickinson's reclusion as an antic disposition, but it *is* made by the authors of this view, Sandra Gilbert and Susan Gubar. It has often been suggested that women poets are particularly prone to suicide — like Plath — and that women tend to be masochistic. It would be female poets who are most prone to begin, in their youth, in gladness, but to come round to grief and madness in the end. The deliberate mutilation of one's own rationality might be a particularly female thing to do. I think not: I tend to distrust this sweeping style of psychological argument, ranking it not too much above the dogmatic diatribes against the possibility of unconditioned female creativity which I dismissed in discussing Ransom's and Hughes's views of Dickinson.

In particular, I am sceptical about the further claim which Gilbert and Gubar make: that a woman novelist may exorcise her authorship anxieties by writing about madwomen, but a woman poet must become a madwoman. This is simply determinism in a novel guise, and a rather naïve view of poetic craft: it tends towards the implication that all poetry is confessional, at least for women. In fact, it comes perilously close to accepting the mad stereotype. And like that myth, it ignores the zest and joyfulness with which Dickinson approached life — and solitude, for the most part. Against the invective addressed to Kate Scott Anthon can be balanced these paeans to solitude:

> The Soul that hath a Guest
> Doth seldom go abroad –
> Diviner Crowd at Home –
> Obliterate the need –
>
> And Courtesy forbid
> A Host's departure when
> Upon himself be visiting
> The Emperor of Men –   (674, *c*. 1863)
>
> The words the happy say
> Are paltry melody
> But those the silent feel
> Are beautiful –   (1750, date unknown)
>
> The reticent volcano keeps
> His never slumbering plan –
> Confided are his projects pink
> To no precarious man.
>
> If nature will not tell the tale
> Jehovah told to her
> Can human nature not survive
> Without a listener?
>
> Admonished by her buckled lips
> Let every babbler be
> The only secret people keep
> Is Immortality.   (1748, date unknown)

On a Columnar Self –
How ample to rely
In Tumult – or Extremity –
How good the Certainty

That Lever cannot pry –
And Wedge cannot divide
Conviction – That Granitic Base –
Though None be on our Side –

Suffice Us – for a Crowd –
Ourself – and Rectitude –
And that Assembly – not far off
From furthest Spirit – God   (789, *c.* 1863)

There is another Loneliness
That many die without –
Not want of friend occasions it
Or circumstance of Lot –

But nature, sometimes, sometimes thought
And whoso it befall
Is richer than could be revealed
By mortal numeral –   (1116, *c.* 1868)

To own the Art within the Soul
The Soul to entertain
With Silence as a Company
And Festival maintain

Is an unfurnished Circumstance
Possession is to One
As an Estate perpetual
Or a reduceless Mine.   (855, *c.* 1864)

No doubt a determined psychoanalytical critic could view all these poems as rationalizations. But that would be as pointless and patronizing as trying to defend this chauvinist view of Dickinson as a helpless compulsive:

[Dickinson] was a private poet who wrote indefatigably, as some women cook or knit. Her gift for words and the cultural predicament of her time drove her to poetry instead of antimacassars.[9]

Neither Dickinson nor her family was as obsessed with her reclusion and its causes as her readers and critics have been. Unless we indulge in sophistry by claiming that her calmness about her own 'lunacy' is proof of that lunacy, we must conclude that a good deal of this particular riddle has been in the eye of the beholder. Jane Donohue Eberwein has pointed out that this tendency to read one's own prejudices or preoccupations into Dickinson's life and work has bedevilled feminists as much as it has holders of the sexist stereotypes about jilting and paternal tyranny.

Whether pitying 'Poor Emily' for her spinsterish seclusion and enshrining her as a sentimental victim of blighted love or assailing her unpublished condition as evidence of the political, social and economic discrimination which stultifies female artistic growth, her modern admirers share Thomas Wentworth Higginson's puzzlement at her ability to make do with so little stimulus or reward — to do without the conditions by which we normally define happiness.[10]

I suggested earlier that Dickinson's isolation eventually harmed her craft, as much as it gave her time to pursue it. The later poems are generally regarded as more difficult than the earlier, although I am not sure that this is anything but another stereotype. But her output did decline as she 'put the belt' of reclusion around her life: she produced only two-thirds the number of poems in her last twenty years that she wrote between 1861 and 1865, when her isolation was not quite so total. Perhaps this is because her failure to publish led to doubts about the worth of the enterprise, and reclusion itself is not to blame — or perhaps the decline in output is only coincidental. Certainly Eberwein claims not only that the reclusion freed Dickinson to write, but that it also freed her writing itself. 'Dickinson herself tightened the screws on each restriction of nineteenth-century norms for women. By her own choice, she immured herself within the magic prison which paradoxically liberated her art.'[11] As she pared her poetry down, abandoning adjectives and sentiment, sometimes omitting necessary connecting words, reducing the natural pentametric rhythm of English to three- and four-beat lines, so she denied herself outside stimulus in order to create an inner silence which would produce her 'letters to the world' — her poems.

> For some – an Ampler Zero –
> A Frost more needle keen
> Is necessary, to reduce
> The Ethiop within . . .　　(430, *c.* 1862)

As self-denying struggle was necessary though not always sufficient for grace to the Puritan, self-denial through isolation was required for poetic development, though it might not be enough. The cocoon of reclusion afforded her the only hope of becoming a butterfly:

> My Cocoon tightens – Colors tease –
> I'm feeling for the Air – . . .　　(1099, *c.* 1866)

The pathos of this poem lies in the constricting effect which the cocoon of silence had upon Dickinson's poetic production, however. In the end one is reminded more of the foot in Neruda's poem, which has the same unlikely ambition, and wonders at the coffin into which it is carried at the last: will it emerge from that chrysalis as a butterfly? To paraphrase Emerson's comment at Thoreau's funeral, in the absence of a vision — and recognition — Dickinson had renounced too much.

In Eberwein's opinion, Dickinson's reclusion was a negative but deliberate and rational choice 'which carried her culture's values for women to an extreme of self-assertion masked as self-effacement'.[12] This is similar to Miller's claim that Dickinson's doubts and timidity were a mask. I have already detailed reasons to doubt that the reclusion took society's values for women and stood them on their head: if Dickinson wanted to flout the expectation that women should lead socially useful lives by exaggerating it, she would have chosen the opposite course to reclusion. Eberwein and Miller tend to accept a rather twentieth-century stereotype of what nineteenth-century Connecticut valley girls were raised up to be. But Eberwein's argument is consistent with Dickinson's character, as was that put forward by Gilbert and Gubar. (It also fits in with the genteel Yankee dictum that character is reflected in the things one does not do.) In youth Dickinson defied her father's insistence that she attend church by the simple ploy of locking herself up in the cellar. Reclusion was also a means of having her own way in later life — as well as a slap in the face for her socially prominent family, who would have expected her to act as their representative at entertainments or on charitable visits. Dickinson was not the 'little home-keeping person' Ransom portrays, but a strong-minded woman.

> The Will it is that situates –
> Equator – never can –   (863, *c.* 1864)

'Masculine in singlemindedness', the modest recluse was actually a monster of wilfulness. The 'little lady in Amherst' turns out to be Rodya Raskolnikov.

> To be alive – is Power –
> Existence – in itself –
> Without a further function–
> Omnipotence – Enough –
>
> To be alive – and Will!
> 'Tis able as a God –
> The Maker – of Ourselves – be what –
> Such being Finitude!   (677, *c.* 1863)

But Dickinson's pride was a wounded pride. Eberwein portrays the reclusion as eminently rational, in an inverted way, and I have already shown reasons why I doubt this. In particular, Eberwein has to claim that Dickinson was content with poetic obscurity as well as personal anonymity, and this is untenable, I think, for reasons I shall discuss at greater length in chapter 6. If Gilbert and Gubar finally come down too much on the side of lunacy in the reclusion, Eberwein is too determined to paint it as entirely sensible. Dickinson's self-imposed isolation was a reasonable reaction to professional failure in a proud woman, but all the same, Dickinson resented her failure, when so many inferior poets came before her eyes every day in the pages of her newspapers and magazines. We are too prone to lose sight of the fact that Dickinson died completely unrecognized because we know how enormous and immediate was her posthumous success. She knew nothing of that when she died, and her life was a tragedy — not because she failed in love, a task she never set herself, but because she was never admitted to the poetic Masonic fraternity. Higginson asked for a photo and details of her age in his reply to her letter about whether her verses 'breathed'; Emerson scoffed that she wrote as if in a fever; Bowles rejected her poems, or printed them anonymously after bowdlerizing them.

If the world would not recognize her, she would refuse to recognize the world. The irony of that would appeal to her humour, and the making the best of a bad situation to her Yankee frugality. Isolation would contract her psychological wants and shrink her stomach for fame. She was forced into reclusion in her art by lack of recognition, but to embrace it in her life was nevertheless a bold and deliberate decision. Once she had 'got a Bomb', the only courageous course was to hold it tight:

> We – could tremble –
> But since we got a Bomb –
> And held it in our Bosom –
> Nay – Hold it – it is calm – (443, *c.* 1862)

I do not think this is too perverse an explanation. It came naturally to a successful woman author, Dickinson's old Amherst acquaintance Emily Fowler Ford:

> I think that in spite of her seclusion, she was longing for poetic sympathy and renown, and that some of her later habits of life originated in this suppressed and ungratified desire of distinction. She wore white, she shut herself away from her race as a mark of her separation from the mass of minds. I only wish the interest and delight her poems have aroused could have come early enough in her career to have kept her social and communicative, and at one with her friends.[13]

Dickinson had to reconcile her image of herself as a professional — which she had to retain if she was to go on imposing any standards on herself in her writing — with her obscurity. Professional failure moulded her personal life. Emily Fowler Ford was able to understand this because she was a professional herself.

Dickinson had a vigorous and generally cheerful disposition, along with a lively wit. But there was a black streak in the wit and a stubbornness in the vigour. Likewise, her reclusion was both grim and gay. We ought not to see it as pitiable, but neither should we lose sight of the tragic in it: the professional failure, the narrowing of subjects and references, the falling-off of creativity, the dying-off of the few remaining friends, and most of all, the frightening side of the adventure into her own hinterlands:

> One need not be a Chamber – to be Haunted–
> One need not be a House –
> The Brain has Corridors – surpassing
> Material Place –
>
> Far safer, of a Midnight Meeting
> External Ghost
> Than its interior Confronting –
> That Cooler Host . . .
>
> Ourself behind ourself, concealed –
> Should startle most –
> Assassin hid in our Apartment
> Be Horror's least . . .   (670, *c*. 1863)
>
> Its Hour with itself
> The Spirit never shows.
> What Terror would enthrall the Street
> Could Countenance disclose
>
> The Subterranean Freight
> The Cellars of the Soul –
> Thank God the loudest Place he made
> Is licensed to be still.   (1225, *c*. 1872)

Silence was an entertainment, as Rich says in 'E.', but it was as much a horror story as a masque.

Dickinson was able to look both the horror and the excitement of the adventure straight in the face, with the near-existential

82

'good faith' I identified in chapter 2. She never turned to religion to comfort her for her professional failure, nor to God as a spiritual companion in her solitude. The myth of the 'New England nun' is exactly back to front in this regard.[14] As Dickinson aged, her reclusion seems to have become more involuntary and burdensome, but her revolt against God deepened. Nevertheless, there is a connection between reclusion and religion in Dickinson: they are linked by that quintessentially fine and private place. The next chapter will elaborate on this connection in death and examine Dickinson's faith and scepticism in greater detail.

Notes

1. Adrienne Rich, 'E.', preface to Gelpi, *Mind*.
2. Eudora Welty, *One Writer's Beginnings* (Cambridge, Mass., and London: Harvard UP, 1984), p. 87.
3. Gelpi, *Mind*, p. 168.
4. Mossberg, *Daughter*, pp. 9, 10.
5. Barbara Welter, *Dimity Convictions: The American Woman in the Nineteenth Century* (Athens, Ohio: Ohio UP, 1976), p. 167.
6. Lydia Sigourney, in Watts, *Poetry of American Women*, p. 91.
7. Gilbert and Gubar, *Madwoman*, p. 586.
8. Ruth Miller, *The Poetry of Emily Dickinson* (Middletown, Conn., Wesleyan UP, 1968), p. 3.
9. R. P. Blackmur, quoted in Gilbert and Gubar, *Madwoman*, p. 543.
10. Jane Donohue Eberwein, 'Doing Without: Dickinson as Yankee Woman Poet', in Ferlazzo (ed.), *Critical Essays*, p. 209.
11. Ibid., pp. 209–10.
12. Ibid., p. 215.
13. Quoted in Sewall, *Life*, vol. 2, p. 378.
14. This phrase, taken from the title of the story I mentioned in chapter 2, was applied to Dickinson by Louis J. Block in an article in *The Dial* (1 March 1895, vol. 18). It has acquired stereotypical connotations which Block himself did not intend: he recognized that Dickinson had a healthy and humourous scepticism about the faith of her fathers.

5 Redemption and Resurrection

The only News I know
Is Bulletins all Day
From Immortality.

The Only Shows I see –
Tomorrow and Today –
Perchance Eternity –

The only One I meet
Is God . . .   (827, *c.* 1864)

Abraham to kill him
Was distinctly told –
Isaac was an Urchin –
Abraham was old –

Not a hesitation –
Abraham complied –
Flattered by Obeisance
Tyranny demurred –

Isaac – to his children
Lived to tell the tale –
Moral – with a Mastiff
Manners may prevail.   (1317, *c.* 1874)

If Dickinson's reclusion enabled her to meet God face to face, she seems to have found the acquaintanceship uncongenial. How can we reconcile these two poems, and what do they tell us about Dickinson's attitude towards religion? Although the New England nun is an inapposite stereotype, Dickinson is often said to have been deeply religious. She is rarely orthodox — despite having been pronounced 'sound' by the family pastor — but redemption, revelation, resurrection, God and Christ are the most frequent themes in her poetry. They are the prime examples of heavy, tormented thoughts tamed and lightened by her typical wit, brevity and scepticism — all underlain by a spirit which has been called intensely sacramental. In part these are simply fruitful, ancient grounds for writing. Dickinson is the first modern poet in most other respects, but she belonged to an age whose writers could still allow themselves religious themes without embarrassment. If Donne had had to contend with a readership which found poems about God and love sentimental, as most modern readers do, his output would have been minuscule. Perhaps the same applies to Dickinson: did she simply use religious themes because she had to make poems, and possessed very little raw material to make them with?

This solution is attractive if we want to emphasize the professional rather than the personal in Dickinson, but it is only a first explanation. After all, religion was *part* of Dickinson's material, her experience — not simply a theme chosen arbitrarily, as a poetic limbering-up exercise. At Mount Holyoke, where mid-century evangelism held sway, the college president Mary Lyon once asked the students to rise if they wanted to admit that they were 'lost' but eager to lead a Christian life. Dickinson was one of the few to remain in her seat. She summarized her reasons: 'They thought it queer I didn't rise — I thought a lie would be queerer'. She was more or less officially branded a 'no-hoper' when she left the college at the end of her first year. Her father, mother, brother and sister were all received into a local church: she never joined, exhibiting that Thoreauvian preference for withdrawing from, rather than joining, organizations. Many of her friends professed conversion during the great waves of revivalism which swept the Connecticut valley during her formative years. She remained sceptical, and resented the breach she sensed in her relations with these girls. Yet she could not abandon belief completely, any more than she could doubt. Puritanism and its transcendental modifications are very evident in her poetry, as chapter 2 showed, even if they are not so dominant as they are sometimes said to be. How, then, did she reconcile belief and doubt in her poems?

The first point to make is that she never reconciled them completely. If anything, the gap between orthodoxy and her private religion grew as she aged. The Kierkegaardean poem about the Abraham and Isaac story was written when she was forty-three (as far as we can be sure about dating any of Dickinson's poems). At about the same time she wrote this resentful, ironic 'justification' of belief:

> Of Heaven above the firmest proof
> We fundamental know
> Except for its marauding Hand
> It had been Heaven below.   (1205, *c.* 1872)

Dickinson refuses to accept that 'by man came death' (I Corinthians 15:21): she blames God. (Later we shall examine whether she can nevertheless maintain a belief in resurrection, which 'by man came also', through the Incarnation.) In 1879 she was still rebelling against God in flippant, atypical rhyming couplets:

> "Heavenly Father" – take to thee
> The supreme iniquity
> Fashioned by thy candid Hand
> In a moment – contraband –
> Though to trust us – seem to us
> More respectful – "We are Dust" –
> We apologise to thee
> For thine own Duplicity –   (1461, *c.* 1879)

In the year before her death she wrote, 'Sustenance is of the spirit/The Gods but dregs' (1623, *c.* 1885). Her Puritan individualism and Emersonian trust in self-reliance actually hamper her belief, as does her Yankee nose for sharp practice:

> Is Heaven an Exchequer?
> They speak of what we owe –
> But that negotiation
> I'm not a Party to –   (1270, *c.* 1873)

'God was penurious with me, which makes me shrewd with him', she once wrote.

But even as she aged and grew away from both God and her evangelical friends, she never became an atheist. That she regards them as a benighted species is clear from this late poem:

How much the present moment means
To those who've nothing more –
The Fop – the Carp – the Atheist –
Stake an entire store
Upon a Moment's shallow Rim. (1380, *c.* 1876)

In her middle age, her doubts extend to her own scepticism:

We shun it ere it comes,
Afraid of Joy,
Then sue it to delay
And lest it fly,
Beguile it more and more –
May not this be,
Old suitor Heaven,
Like our dismay at thee? (1580, *c.* 1882)

She professes that she still wants to love God, even though He
requires her to put away her affection for this world:

My Maker – let me be
Enamored most of thee –
But nearer this
I more should miss –   (1403, c. 1877)

But God turns His face away, and her faith in immortality
weakens when she needs it most, as her family and friends die off
and she herself ages:

Those – dying then,
Knew where they went –
They went to God's Right Hand –
That Hand is amputated now
And God cannot be found –

The abdication of Belief
Makes the behaviour small –
Better an ignis fatuus
Than no illume at all –   (1551, *c.* 1882)

Lives he in any other world
My faith cannot reply
Before it was imperative
'Twas all distinct to me –   (1557, *c.* 1882)

'This is the hour of lead' in Dickinson's religious poetry: the moment of near-existential despair. Yet her humour is also at its sharpest in her religious poems. Perhaps it is more typical in her earlier poetry, and the scepticism it serves a more affordable luxury to the younger woman. 'Dust is the only Secret' (*c.*1860) was reproduced in part in chapter 2, where I presented it as a satire on the New England virtues of industry and frugality. In the same poem Dickinson whimsically describes Christ as the robber who undermines the prudent efforts of the good burgher, Death, by smuggling souls to Heaven. Another early poem mocks revivalism by calling it an opiate of the masses:

Much gesture, from the Pulpit –
Strong Hallelujahs roll –
Narcotics cannot still the Tooth
That nibbles at the soul –   (501, *c.* 1862)

More often her humour is less broad, more ironic: but it is always used in the service of scepticism.

It's easy to invent a Life –
God does it – every Day –
Creation – but the Gambol
Of His Authority –

It's easy to efface it –
The thrifty Deity
Could scarce afford Eternity
To Spontaneity –   (724, *c.* 1863)

It is an honorable Thought
And makes One lift One's Hat
As one met sudden Gentlefolk
Upon a daily Street

That We've immortal Place
Though Pyramids decay
And Kingdoms, like the Orchard
Flit Russetly away   (946, c. 1864)

And after *that*– there's Heaven –
The *Good* Man's – "Dividend" –
And *Bad* Men – "go to Jail"–
I guess –   (234, *c.* 1861)

Whimsy, business metaphor and the family hauteur combine
in this broadside against the 'rival claims' of the revivalists, who
endanger Dickinson's valued privacy:

I had some things that I called mine –
And God, that he called his,
Till, recently a rival Claim
Disturbed these amities.

The property, my garden,
Which having sown with care,
He claims the pretty acre
And sends a Bailiff there.

The station of the parties
Forbids publicity,
But Justice is sublimer
Than arms, or pedigree.

I'll institute an "Action" –
I'll vindicate the law –
Jove! Choose your counsel –
I retain "Shaw"!   (116, *c.* 1859)

Perhaps the weakness and obscurity of the last line may explain
why this revealing poem is so little known. Or perhaps its
assertive heresy was judged improper by Todd, who promulgated
a harmless and orthodox image of Dickinson in her readings and
lecture tours. In any case, this poem, which did not appear in
print till 1945, epitomizes Dickinson's concern for privacy in

religious matters. She was reclusive even from God, whom she regarded as merely her peer. (Note that she classes herself as the Deity's equal in the line, 'The station of the parties' — parties in the plural.) Reverence towards superior power is foreign to her nature, reverent though she is towards nature and the inner self. In another early poem, 'Should you but fail at sea' (c. 1861), she declares she would *'harass God'* (underlined in the original) until he admitted her loved one to Paradise. Pride and will — ignored in the stereotype of Dickinson as the scorned victim of unrequited love or the miserable prisoner of the tyrannical father — are always to the fore in Dickinson's religious poetry, as in most of her poems.

> To be alive – and Will!
> 'Tis able as a God –
> The Maker – of Ourselves – be what –
> Such being Finitude!   (677, c. 1863)

She asserted, 'To be human is more than to be divine, for when Christ was divine, he was uncontented till he had been human'. It is little wonder Dickinson thought it a lie to acknowledge herself as lost but eager to be saved. In a profound sense, the self is never lost in her poetry: over 130 poems begin with 'I', and more with 'my' and 'myself'. She is an assertive individualist who can worship but not pray — especially not to 'that bold Person, God' (900).

Part of the answer to my initial query — how we can reconcile Dickinson's 'religious' inwardness with her resentment of God — is that Dickinson ultimately excludes God from her religion. She is willing to admit Christ, although he is required to address her from behind a half-closed door. He is an acceptable visitor because his calling card is engraved 'Son of Man'. In a letter of 1873 she wrote: 'The loveliest sermon I ever heard was the disappointment of Jesus in Judas. It was told like a mortal story of intimate young men'. A letter of eleven years later maintained the same attitude: 'When Jesus tells us about his Father, we distrust him. When he shows us his Home, we turn away, but when he confides to us that he is "acquainted with Grief", we listen, for that is also an Acquaintance of our own'. God is so small a part of Dickinson's religion that she can declare Christ achieved resurrection through his own self-reliant efforts:

> Obtaining but our own Extent
> In whatsoever Realm –
> 'Twas Christ's own personal Expanse
> That bore him from the Tomb –   (1543, *c.* 1882)

And a principal task Christ imposed on himself was reclusion:

> To put this World down, like a Bundle –
> And walk steady, away,
> Requires Energy – possibly Agony –
> 'Tis the Scarlet way
>
> Trodden with straight renunciation
> By the Son of God . . .   (527, *c.* 1862)

Redemption through the active imitation of Christ (more than through passive acceptance of Christ's intervention, resembling 'charity' as that does) is one component of Dickinson's religious belief. It is beautifully embodied in this difficult poem which combines the themes of religion and reclusion:

> Till Death – is narrow Loving –
> The scantest Heart extant
> Will hold you till your privilege
> Of Finiteness – be spent –
>
> But He whose loss procures you
> Such Destitution that
> Your Life too abject for itself
> Thenceforward imitate –
>
> Until – Resemblance perfect –
> Yourself, for His pursuit
> Delight of Nature – abdicate –
> Exhibit Love – somewhat –   (907, *c.* 1864)

There is little evidence in this poem of the primitiveness of which both her writing and her theology have been accused, especially by her earliest and most patronizing critics. This poem is a complicated statement which I can only construe in part. I would paraphrase it this way: Anyone can love or be loved until death, but Christ's loss to us was so great that we must go on loving him after his death. The only compensation we can offer ourselves for his loss is an ironic destitution: the ascetic imitation of Christ. This is the only true meaning of love, but even this is not enough. Dickinson says it better, even with the missed connectives.

But Dickinson loves the world too much to pursue Christ in this ascetic way. Her own 'renunciation of the world' through reclusion was partly inadvertent, as I have shown in the previous chapter, and to that extent it was a 'destitution'. But she also saw it as a fruitful and joyful turning inwards, a confronting of the essential, a search for the place where 'consciousness is Noon'. Throughout this book I have tried to portray Dickinson as 'one of the great daughters of Joy', to paraphrase Wagenknecht's comment on Thoreau. She took too much pleasure in her world, dry though it seems to us, to tread any 'Scarlet way' of renunciation, even for redemption's sake. The old Puritan doubts about the certainty of grace combine with her ironic scepticism to make her question whether redemption really exists.

> Which is best? Heaven –
> Or only Heaven to come
> With that old codicil of Doubt?
> I cannot help esteem
> The "Bird within the Hand"
> Superior to the one
> The "Bush" may yield me
> Or may not
> Too late to choose again.   (1012, *c*. 1865)

This poem reverses Pascal's Wager, which counsels doubters to follow God's commandments even if they are unsure whether the afterlife exists. If there is any chance at all that Hell awaits the unjust and Heaven the virtuous, the penalities and rewards to be had are infinitely great, but the sacrifice of worldly pleasure only finite.

> Do not hesitate then [*advises Pascal*] wager that [God] does exist . . . [for] there is an infinity of infinitely happy life to be won, one chance of winning against a finite number of chances of losing, and what you are staking is finite. That leaves no choice: wherever there is infinity, and where there are not infinite chances of losing against that of winning, there is no room for hesitation, you must give everything.[1]

Dickinson is rarely willing to give everything, and cannot help doubting. But her scepticism here extends even to her own choice of this world over the next. She knows she may change her mind later, but she recognizes that by then it will be too late for redemption. There is a tragic awareness in Dickinson, but it has nothing to do with the 'tragedy' of spinsterhood.

Redemption through Christ is one component of Dickinson's belief, then, but it is vitiated by scepticism. The same is true of resurrection, which plays a greater part in her theology. Immortality and eternity are constantly recurring themes in her poems — although frequently they are only 'buzz-words', imposing terms chosen to end a poem grandly or to balance the brevity and choppy scansions of her lines. The poem with which this chapter began, 'The only News I know', uses 'immortality', 'eternity', and very likely 'God' in this manner, to suit the requirements of the craft. The usefulness of these 'religious' terms for purely aesthetic and professional purposes goes some way towards explaining why Dickinson appears to be so obsessed with religion, even though she has so little time for God. In one of her best-known poems, 'immortality' and 'eternity' are again used as buzz-words, crucially positioned at the end of the first and last stanzas. Orthodox belief in resurrection and judgement is conspicuous by its lack:

> Because I could not stop for Death –
> He kindly stopped for me –
> The Carriage held but just Ourselves –
> And Immortality.
>
> We slowly drove – He knew no haste
> And I had put away
> My labor and my leisure, too,
> For His Civility –

We passed the School, where Children strove
At Recess – in the Ring –
We passed the Fields of Gazing Grain –
We passed the Setting Sun –

Or rather – He passed Us –
The Dews drew quivering and chill –
For only Gossamer, my Gown –
My Tippet – only Tulle –

We paused before a House that seemed
A Swelling of the Ground –
The Roof was scarcely visible –
The Cornice – in the Ground –

Since then – 'tis Centuries – and yet
Feels shorter than the Day
I first surmised the Horses' Heads
Were toward Eternity –   (712, *c.* 1863)

All the mortuary poetry of Dickinson's time vouchsafed an after-life: a reward for suffering, a refuge for the little angels who died in childhood. Dickinson stops at the grave and goes no further, though she has all of eternity in which to travel on.

When Dickinson does bring up resurrection, she does so with her usual empirical scepticism. Writing to the Reverend Higginson after her father's death, she was conventional and polite enough towards a man of the cloth to assure him, 'I am glad there is Immortality'. But she qualified her belief with this modifier: '[I] would have tested it myself before entrusting him'. In this poem she sounds the more typical note of snobbery combined with uncertainty:

The Fact that Earth is Heaven –
Whether Heaven is Heaven or not
If not an Affidavit
Of that specific Spot
Not only must confirm us
That it is not for us
But that it would affront us
To dwell in such a place –   (1408, *c.* 1877)

What belief Dickinson does maintain in the afterlife is inferred from natural scientific grounds, in a rationalistic, transcendental manner. Like the Russian poet Andrei Vosnesenskii, she finds more material for a speculatively minded poet in science than anywhere else. Like Thoreau, she infers 'Heaven above' from 'Heaven below': 'No higher heaven than the pure senses can furnish, a *purely* sensuous life. . . . May we not *see* God?'[2] It takes a scientific metaphor, the law of the conservation of matter, to convince Dickinson of the resurrection of the body:

> The Chemical conviction
> That Nought be lost
> Enable in Disaster
> My fractured Trust –
>
> The Faces of the Atoms
> If I shall see
> How more the Finished Creatures
> Departed me!   (954, *c.* 1864)

But Dickinson's language betrays her doubts. 'Enable' in the third line is probably no grammatical mistake, but a subjunctive, with the meaning 'let it enable' or 'might enable'. (This is a form she uses frequently, and I shall explore the confusion it has caused in the next chapter.) Similarly, the 'if' in the second line of the second stanza reflects uncertainty. If there is any belief to be had, induction will have to provide it: but it may be unable to. Ultimately the paradoxes of resurrection are beyond rational belief:

> To die – without the Dying
> And live – without the Life –
> This is the hardest Miracle
> Propounded to Belief.   (1017, *c.* 1865)

As greatly as she wants to believe in immortality, she cannot help doubting, and the doubts deepen as she ages.

> The Spirit lasts – but in what mode –
> Below, the Body speaks,

But as the Spirit furnishes –
Apart, it never talks –
The Music in the Violin
Does not emerge alone
But arm in arm with Touch, yet Touch
Alone – is not a Tune –   (1576, *c.* 1883)

Ultimately, even immortality is an invasion of privacy, and an occasion for wit:

The right to perish might be thought
An undisputed right –
Attempt it, and the Universe
Upon the opposite
Will concentrate its officers –
You cannot even die
But nature and mankind must pause
To pay you scrutiny.   (1692, date unknown)

But there is one kind of immortality which Dickinson never rejected: the sort she found mentioned in the essay of Higginson's which prompted her to ask him whether her poems 'breathed'. In that article, 'Letter to a Young Contributor', Higginson — 'muscular Christian' though his friends called him — had written 'A book is the only immortality', quoting Choate. This was the resurrection after death in which Dickinson believed most fervently. She died convinced that it had been denied her.

Notes

1. Blaise Pascal, *Pensées*, II (1684; Harmondsworth: Penguin Books, 1966), pp. 151–2.
2. Thoreau, quoted in Gelpi, *Mind*, p. 78.

6 Recognition

When Emily Dickinson died in 1886, she had published only seven poems, all anonymously. Five years later, the first book of her poems went through six printings in six months. Twelve years after her death, she was translated into German, and her poems have now appeared in nineteen languages. During her lifetime Higginson scolded her for her 'spasmodic' poetic gait, and Bowles condescended to her poems as 'little gems'. By the 1920s she had metamorphosed into the greatest woman poet in the English language, in the opinion of one critic who will be considered later. Poe was without honour in his native country, although fashionable in France; Thoreau was regarded as little better than the captain of a huckleberrying party; Hawthorne was esteemed by other authors but not bought by the public; Melville achieved popular success with his early lighter works but not with the major ones; Whitman achieved mainly a *succès de scandale*. No nineteenth-century American writer except perhaps Twain or Emerson was regarded in the same critical light in his own time as now: yet at least they *saw* the light of publication. Dickinson is unique: complete professional failure in life, runaway success after death. How did this happen? And did her failure matter to Dickinson? Anyone looking for a good story is bound to be disappointed by the meagre facts of Dickinson's life, but enthralled by the odd tale of the poems' publication. This is where the interest, irony and tragedy lie: not in the non-existent love life or the reasonably harmonious family relations.

Dickinson was writing intensely by the early 1860s, as the handwriting evidence demonstrates. Whether she wrote a great deal before this prolific period is unclear. She claimed in her April 1862 letter to Higginson to have begun writing only the previous winter; but she was a proud woman, prone to posing, who might have wanted to hide her failure to publish if she *had* been writing longer. Some 300 poems are generally dated earlier than 1862, and it seems quite certain that she began assembling the 'fascicles' of eighteen to twenty poems each in about 1858. Some commentators claim that she began writing poetry in the early

1850s, following on from her high reputation in school and college composition. This seems likely: it takes time to develop one's own poetic voice, and Dickinson had found hers in the earliest poems we possess, dated to the late 1850s. Perhaps she threw away her youthful apprentice work, the early poetic peccadilloes. Dickinson might have been referring to writing poetry in this strange confession of her twentieth year: 'I have dared to do strange things – bold things, and have asked no advice from any – I have heeded beautiful tempters, yet do not think I am wrong'. She was living quietly at home when she wrote this letter to a friend in 1850, and there is no record of any external 'beautiful tempters'. But there was enough of Puritanism left in her environment — particularly with the admixture of fundamentalism and revivalism — to brand writing as a guilty occupation. Dickinson was educated to regard Pope as a rake, Shakespeare as a libertine, and Voltaire, Hume and Gibbon as atheists. She never read Whitman because she was told that his poems were shocking. With such attitudes around her, she might well have felt fearful about acknowledging her vocation. Hawthorne expressed guilt about his, and he lacked the additional handicap of being female. Women were expected to plead economic necessity if they turned to a literary living.

There were, however, many women poets in Dickinson's time. It is simply incorrect to view Dickinson's failure to publish as straightforward repression of all women writers. But the women poets were of a particular dying breed. In the early nineteenth century an enormous amount of verse was written by women for women in America, and lady's magazines flourished. It has been said that it was actually easier for a woman to publish poetry at this time than it was for a man.[1] Lydia Huntley Sigourney, the 'Sweet Singer of Hartford', was the first American poet of either sex who was able to support herself and her family through her verse. Elizabeth Oakes Smith and Frances Sargent Osgood made considerable reputations. The English writer, Felicia Hemans — best remembered for her poem about 'the stately homes of England' — was enormously popular in America. Feminism was further advanced than in England. Some women editors held great power: the women's rights advocate Margaret Fuller at the *Dial*, Sarah Josepha Hale at *Godey's Lady's Book*.

But by the time Dickinson was ready to publish, this distaff intelligentsia was either dead or under concerted cannon-fire from male writers and editors, Longfellow, Emerson and Hawthorne among them. In *Huckleberry Finn* Mark Twain mocks the prevalent heroic dirge style through the character of Emmeline Grangerford, the precociously maudlin authoress of funeral elegies, who pined away and died young when she was unable to find a rhyme for a particularly troublesome corpse named Whistler. A 'typical' Grangerford poem is parodied as follows:

Ode to Stephen Dowling Bots, Dec'd

And did young Stephen sicken,
And did young Stephen die?
And did the sad hearts thicken,
And did the mourners cry?

No: such was not the fate of
Young Stephen Dowling Bots,
Though sad hearts round him thickened,
'Twas not from sickness' shots.

No whooping-cough did rack his frame,
Nor measles drear with spots;
Not these impaired the sacred name
Of Stephen Dowling Bots.

Despised love struck not with woe
That head of curly knots
Nor stomach troubles laid him low,
Young Stephen Dowling Bots.

O no. Then list with tearful eye,
Whilst I his fate do tell.
His soul did from this cold world fly
By falling down a well.

They got him out and emptied him;
Alas it was too late;
His spirit was gone for to sport aloft
In the realms of the good and great.[2]

Women's poetry was branded as restricted and sentimental, and the magazines which began to establish the canon of great names — the *Atlantic Monthly*, *Scribner's*, *Knickerbocker's* — printed few poems by women. Opprobrium was heaped on women writers who wrote under their maiden names, a sin only slightly less mortal than the practice some women had actually indulged in of writing without their husbands' permission. By the middle of the century, masculine revanchism was so far advanced that Higginson felt called upon to pen a satirical article, 'Ought Women to Learn the Alphabet?'

But even if it is untrue that Dickinson failed to publish because no women poets were or ever had been published, the poetry which other women wrote was quite unlike hers — as was the poetry men wrote, for that matter. She would have laughed to scorn the idea of making a reputation as the Sweet Singer of Amherst — or worse still of nearby Chicopee or Belchertown. The poetry by women which Bowles featured in the *Republican*, sometimes called the New England *Manchester Guardian*, tended to rigor mortis. So did men's, of course, as this poem by one William Winter shows:

The Last Scene

Here she lieth, white and chill;
Put your hand upon her brow;
For her heart is very still,
And she does not know you now.

Ah! the grave's a quiet bed!
She shall sleep a pleasant sleep,
And the tears that you may shed,
Will not wake her — therefore weep.

Weep — for you have wrought her woe;
Mourn — she mourned and died for you;
Ah, too late we come to know
What is false and what is true.[3]

Bowles prided himself on featuring intellectual ladies, but they were required to conform to the same moribund standards. By

1890 the popular taste may have changed, if Dickinson sold so well. But that mid-century preferences were bleaker is clear from Bowles's introduction to the poem 'Over the River' by Nancy A. W. Priest. Of this he, or his associate Josiah Gilbert Holland, wrote: 'Such is the renewed interest in this sweet and touching poem, by our correspondent, Miss Nancy A. W. Priest of Hinsdale, N.H., that we can only supply the constant demand for copies by a second re-publication'.

Over the River

Over the river they beckon to me —
Loved ones who've crossed to the further side;
The gleam of their snowy robes I see,
But their voices are drowned in the rushing tide.
There's one with ringlets of sunny gold,
And eyes, the reflection of heaven's own blue;
He crossed in twilight, grey and cold,
And the pale mist hid him from mortal view.
We saw not the angels who met him there;
The gate of the city we could not see;
Over the river, over the river,
My brother stands waiting to welcome me! . . .[4]

The real riddle in Emily Dickinson's life is how she managed to avoid writing like this. We now think it was design, genius, a unique and unconventional craftsmanship. The editors of her time — and the critics who reviewed the 1890 volume, especially the English ones — thought it was incompetence. In the end Bowles printed five of her poems, all without credit, whilst names which are now forgotten graced his pages. When he did publish her work, he tinkered with it. Dickinson complained that he had 'robbed' her of 'A narrow fellow in the grass' because he altered the punctuation — a quibble, it might seem, but actually a sign of her professional craftsmanship. Bowles went further with 'I taste a liquor never brewed'. He added his own title, 'The May-Wine', and changed the half-rhymes — which were also derided thirty years later by Andrew Lang and other critics — from pearl/ alcohol to pearl/whirl, so that the first verse ended 'Nor Frankfort berries yield the sense/Such a delirious whirl'. The stagy 'nor' and the conscious use of a deliberately 'poetic' term, 'delirious', delineate the difference between Dickinson's and the popular style.

Dickinson got roughly nowhere by trying to exploit the family connection with Bowles. But she was ambitious and bold enough to write directly to a literary lion she did not know, Thomas Wentworth Higginson, after she had read his article, 'Letter to a Young Contributor', in the *Atlantic Monthly* of April 1862. Higginson was a man of letters who had begun his career as a radical abolitionist: a member of the 'Secret Six' who conspired with John Brown in planning the Harper's Ferry raid. He had been wounded in defending the fugitive slave Anthony Burns from recapture and was soon to take up a commission as colonel of a black regiment. He also had a considerable reputation as a friend of literary women, as witness his satirical essay in their defence, 'Ought Women to Learn the Alphabet?'.

But Higginson's dedication to the women's cause did not prevent him from answering Dickinson's request for professional help with a request for a picture and a question about how old she was. (This was the request which occasioned the comment printed as an introductory quotation to this book.) Nor was he encouraging or tactful about her quirky poems. The day after he received Dickinson's letter, he rounded jestingly on the *Atlantic*'s editor for exposing him to talentless and importunate authors: 'Two such specimens of verse as came yesterday and the day before — fortunately *not* to be forwarded for publication'. The other hopeful is forgotten, and so might 'the greatest woman poet' have been if Higginson had been left to his own devices — in which case Higginson too would be forgotten. He called Dickinson's metres 'spasmodic' and 'uncontrolled' in his reply to her, even though she had included such carefully honed poems as 'Safe in their Alabaster Chambers'. And he warned her that she was by no means ready to publish.

Dickinson's answer of 7 June 1862 is famous:

I smile when you suggest that I delay "to publish" – that being foreign to my thought, as Firmament to Fin – If Fame belonged to me, I could not escape her – if she did not, the longest day would pass me on the chase – and the approbation of my Dog, would forsake me – then – my barefoot – Rank is better.

This disavowal has often been taken at face value and used to shore up the shy genius myth. But the comment is ambiguous: it might mean that Dickinson would go on chasing fame for as long as it was denied her. In any case, it takes very little reading between the lines to surmise that the lady doth protest too much. The letter fairly oozes hurt pride, offended Dickinson hauteur, and sour grapes — as well it might. Higginson had made bold to criticize the woman who wrote:

> That she forgot me was the least
> I felt it second pain
> That I was worthy to forget
> Was most I thought upon –   (1683, date unknown)

Dickinson could barely control her outrage with her usual wit: 'You think my gait "spasmodic" – I am in danger – Sir – You think me "uncontrolled" – I have no tribunal'. She offers a mock apology for her foolhardiness in coming to the great man for advice that proved insensitive: 'Myself the only Kangaroo among the Beauty, Sir, if you please, it afflicts me, and I thought that instruction would take it away'.

'The only Kangaroo among the Beauty' — what can Dickinson mean but that she is the solitary wallflower at the Bowles co-tillion? How can there be any doubt that she resents her failure to publish? Why would she have sent Higginson her poems in the first place if she were entirely content with her 'barefoot rank'? This was the forthright act of an ambitious woman, though not one who would condescend to make her requests outright. A combination of shyness and peremptoriness typified her, as it did Vinnie, who browbeat Mabel Todd into frequent visits to publishers whom she was too reclusive to visit herself. Hoping that Higginson might eventually take the hint, Dickinson went on sending him poems throughout her lifetime, to a total of over one hundred, none of which he 'forwarded for publication'.

Nevertheless, it is a mistake to paint Higginson as the villain of Dickinson's undoubted professional tragedy. We would be un-likely to have the poems today if he had not acceded to Todd's less dictatorial and simultaneously more forthright requests in 1890. And Dickinson herself wrote to Higginson that he had 'saved her life'. Perhaps she meant that at least he was less patronizing about her work than Bowles, that he took her seriously. Tactless though he was, he did reply to her letters and continue the correspondence until her death. He invited her to his literary gatherings in Boston and, when she refused on the grounds of her reclusion, visited her in Amherst on two occasions. He took the trouble to record her now-famous comment at their first meeting: 'If I read a book [and] it makes my whole body feel so cold no fire can ever warm me, I know *that* is poetry. If I feel physically as if the top of my head were taken off, I know *that* is poetry. These are the only ways I know it. Is there any other way?' All this he did despite his wife's mournful conviction that Dickinson was insane, and a leech with it. Dickinson's poems *were* deeply unconventional and difficult to judge. Even by 1890 critical opinion was still largely damning — though the public was worshipful — and Higginson was thought very incautious to have sponsored the poems. Dickinson was modern half a century before Hardy, and no publisher or editor was 'ready' for her.

By the mid-1860s Dickinson had given up on Bowles, and Higginson was proving friendly but unhelpful. She was able to publish one poem in her Sweetser cousins' newspaper — 'Some keep the Sabbath going to Church'. But the next record we have of her continued attempts to publish in a major magazine comes from Emily Fowler Ford, Dickinson's childhood acquaintance who opined later that the reclusion originated in a suppressed urge for recognition. Ford was a successful literary figure by the 1870s when she was approached for an opinion on Dickinson's poems by Holland, by then editor of *Scribner's Magazine*. Dickinson had sent some of her work to Holland — another family friend, though also the author of a fable moralizing about women authors — but he remained sceptical. Ford records the conversation as proceeding in this manner:

Holland: You know Emily Dickinson. I have some poems of hers under consideration for publication — but they are not really suitable — they are too ethereal.
Ford: They are beautiful, so concentrated, but they remind me of orchids, air-plants that have no roots in earth.
Holland: That is true — a perfect description. I dare not use them.

This is a sad little dialogue because it was Ford who later

identified lack of professional recognition as a prime cause of Dickinson's eccentricities. And it is particularly ironic in that this judgement damns Dickinson for exactly the opposite faults which were found in her work when it *was* published after her death. Higginson's ambivalent introduction to the *Poems* of 1890 took Dickinson to task for having too *much* of earth about her: 'Her verses are in most cases like poetry plucked up by the roots; we have them with earth, stones and dew adhering, and must accept them as they are'. Critics of that time rounded on her lack of lyricism, her failure to be 'ethereal' enough.

Dickinson came nearest to professional success through the ministrations of her old acquaintance Helen Hunt Jackson, a successful novelist and another protégée of Higginson's. Jackson was convinced that Dickinson was a great poet, and she did her best to prod her out of her shell of personal reclusion and poetic obscurity. In the 1870s anonymous volumes were in vogue, and Jackson's acquaintance, the editor Thomas Niles, was preparing a book of contributions by anonymous poets for his 'No Name' series. Jackson arranged for Dickinson's 'Success is Counted Sweetest' to be included in this book, *A Masque of Poets*, although even this poem was edited for its own good. This is how it runs in the original:

> Success is counted sweetest
> By those who ne'er succeed
> To comprehend a nectar
> Requires sorest need.
>
> Not one of all the purple Host
> Who took the Flag today
> Can tell the definition
> So clear of Victory
>
> As he defeated – dying –
> On whose forbidden ear
> The distant strains of triumph
> Burst agonized and clear!

This is the version edited by Niles:

Success is counted sweetest
By those that ne'er succeed
To comprehend a nectar
Requires the sorest need.

Not one of all the purple Host
Who took the Flag today
Can tell the definition
So plain of Victory

As he defeated – dying
On whose forbidden ear
The distant strains of triumph
Break, agonizing clear.

These are small changes, but on a miniature canvas, little slips of the brush make a great deal of difference. The overall effect of Niles's 'improvements' is to trivialize and flatten the poem: the trite 'break' for 'burst', the pretentious bathos of 'agonizing clear'. The amendments do not even improve Dickinson's grammar, atrocious though later critics claimed that to be. She is grammatically correct to use 'who' in the second line of the first stanza: 'that' serves no purpose but alliteration — which Dickinson was often accused of using in excess, ironically enough, since it was her editor who went for it here. 'Agonized and clear' is a perfectly correct pair of predicate adjectives; in Niles's version, 'agonizing' should be 'agonizingly', an adverb. The changes are petty, but petty-minded: they lessen the poem's originality without improving on its perfectly clear meaning and sound grammar.

Nevertheless Niles was sufficiently impressed with Dickinson's work, even with these 'warts', to ask her for a manuscript of her poems in 1883. This is the most apparently puzzling episode in the history of Dickinson's attempts at publication: she never sent him one, although she kept up the correspondence and sent many individual poems. Does this indicate that I have been wrong to call her a professional-minded and ambitious writer? Is the shy genius myth correct after all? I think not: by 1883 Dickinson was fifty-two years old and largely resigned to her obscurity — or afraid of getting her hopes up again. In addition, she was buffeted by overwhelming personal losses. This was the year in which her much-loved eight-year-old nephew died, Austin had malaria, and Vinnie was also ill. In late 1882 Dickinson's mother had died. Judge Lord, her most serious lover, had a stroke in 1883 and died the following March. In June 1884 Dickinson had a nervous breakdown, dying two years later. Helen Hunt Jackson died in 1885, and Niles's admiration for Dickinson's work seems to have passed with her. When Todd visited Niles's office in 1890 he told her that 'to publish [Dickinson's] "lucubrations" had always seemed to him "most undesirable"'. The offer to publish may have been made reluctantly, under Jackson's determined urging. At any rate, by 1890 Niles was denying it had ever existed.

This exhausts the record of Dickinson's attempts to publish. Perhaps she should have tried harder, approaching more editors outside the circle of her family and friends. But then again, perhaps she did: she was brave enough with Higginson. And perhaps she received the nineteenth-century equivalent of form rejection slips, which she would have had no reason to save. We have very little of her total correspondence, and editors whom she did not know personally would have been very unlikely to have kept a record of unsolicited manuscripts from a provincial woman. Whether or not she made other attempts, we cannot know: but we do know that Todd, an attractive, sophisticated and determined woman, practically had to camp out in Boston editors' offices before she was able to place the poems. When she finally did manage to arrange publication, it was on a 'vanity' basis. Dickinson would never have been allowed to pay for her poems' publication in her father's lifetime, and she had no independent income. It was one thing for Vinnie to pay for publication later, as a memorial to her sister, but another for Emily to spend money on her 'vanity'; in any case, authorial pride would have been as sensitive about vanity publishing as it is now — and pride was the moving force of Dickinson's disposition. The claim that Dickinson chose not to publish assumes that she had only to pick up her magic wand.

What evidence we possess makes it clear that Dickinson wanted to publish, although she grew disheartened and perhaps a bit lethargic about professional success as she aged. This historical record seems to be at odds with Dickinson's poems, however, many of which eschew ambition — or try to. Such poems as

'Publication is the Auction' are often cited to uphold Higginson's singularly obtuse claim that Dickinson never sought to publish.

> Publication – is the Auction
> Of the Mind of Man –
> Poverty – be justifying
> For so foul a thing
>
> Possibly – but We – would rather
> From our Garret go
> White – Unto the White Creator –
> Than invest – our Snow –
>
> Thought belong to Him who gave it –
> Then – to Him who bear
> Its Corporeal illustration – Sell
> The Royal Air –
>
> In the Parcel – Be the Merchant
> Of the Heavenly Grace –
> But reduce no Human Spirit
> To Disgrace of Price –   (709, c. 1863)

Why not take this poem at face value? For one thing, Dickinson's actions spoke louder than her words: she did expose her works to editors and belletrists and that fact gives rise to the suspicion that this poem, like the disclaimer in her letter to Higginson, is 'sour grapes'. It is dated — roughly, to be sure — just after the time when Bowles had played down her work and Higginson patronized it. But this poem also reflects the pressures which nineteenth-century New England society brought to bear against respectable women who had literary aspirations. As I have mentioned, there were female authors, but they were expected to plead widowhood or husbandly financial mismanagement, as did Helen Hunt Jackson and Lydia Sigourney. ('Poverty – be justifying/For so foul a thing.') Cautionary tales were printed for aspiring women writers who had no economic need to seek success. Josiah Holland, co-editor of the *Springfield Republican* and husband of one of Dickinson's girlhood friends, published one of these, *Miss Gilbert's Career*. Like the English anti-feminist homilies which gloated over Wollstonecraft's death in childbirth as a sign to dissatisfied women, these fables were filled with didactic proselytizing. They warned how indecent it was for a woman to 'print her soul' — a phrase which Dickinson picked up from Elizabeth Barrett Browning, ironically enough, and used in a dilatory letter to Helen Hunt Jackson. Dickinson was conventional in many respects — in her choice of poetic themes, for example, or in her acceptance of Whitman as inappropriate reading. The poem 'Publication is the Auction' reflects the tension she must have felt between her own ambition and society's disapproval — with more than a hint of whistling in the dark and posing, particularly in the line about her 'Garret', the best bedroom!

But how else do we know that Dickinson *was* ambitious — apart from the publishing attempts? As a girl, she was heard by the family seamstress to say, 'When I die, they'll have to remember me' — an unintentional bit of irony, since she was forgotten *during* her lifetime. This story may be apocryphal, another piece of myth-making, but there is a letter written to her cousin Louise Norcross in 1858 which speculates on fame. Recalling a girlhood conversation, she reminds Louise of the time 'you and I . . . decided to be distinguished. It's a great thing to be "great", Loo, and you and I might try for a life, and never accomplish it, but no one can stop our looking on, and you know some cannot sing, but the orchard is full of birds, and we can all listen. What if we learn, ourselves, some day? Who indeed knows?' The tone of this letter is more modest than we would expect of an ambitious woman, but perhaps that can be explained by Dickinson's characteristic light manner and by the letter's date. She was not in the full spate of her writing by this time, and any speculations on poetic fame would have been empty.

Most telling, apart from the actual search for a publisher, is the number of poems Dickinson wrote about fame. Many claim to want to have nothing to do with success, in the typically Emersonian self-sufficient manner, but the *topic* of fame could not be renounced so easily. Throughout her writing life Dickinson returned to professional recognition as a theme:

> Some – Work for Immortality –
> The Chiefer part, for Time –

He – Compensates – immediately –
The former – Checks – on Fame –

Slow Gold – but Everlasting –
The Bullion of Today –
Contrasted with the Currency –
Of Immortality –

A Beggar – Here and There –
Is gifted to discern –
Beyond the Broker's insight –
One's – Money – One's – the Mine –   (406, *c.* 1862)

Fame of Myself, to justify,
All other Plaudit be
Superfluous – An Incense
Beyond Necessity –

Fame of Myself to lack – Although
My Name be else Supreme –
This were an Honor honorless –
A futile Diadem –   (713, *c.* 1863)

All men for Honor hardest work
But are not known to earn –
Paid after they have ceased to work
In Infamy or Urn –   (1193, *c.* 1871)

The Beggar at the Door for Fame
Were easily supplied
But Bread is that Diviner thing
Disclosed to be denied   (1240, *c.* 1872)

Praise it – 'tis dead –
It cannot glow –
Warm this inclement Ear
With the encomium it earned
Since it was gathered here –
Invest this alabaster Zest
In the Delights of Dust –

Remitted – since it flitted it
In recusance august.   (1384, *c.* 1876)

Fame is the one that does not stay –   .
Its occupant must die
Or out of sight of estimate
Ascend incessantly –

Or be that most insolvent thing
A Lightning in the Germ –
Electrical the embryo
But we demand the Flame   (1475, *c.* 1879)

These poems suggest that Dickinson went on demanding the
'Flame' of fame: her frequent returns to the topic of success
indicate that she never accepted her lack of reputation. But
although we commonly take publication to be the mark of the
professional rather than the Sunday poet, we need not prove that
Dickinson wanted fame in order to regard her as a professional.
The evidence confirms that she *did* dwell on fame in her thoughts
and seek recognition in her actions. But even if she had not, she
still has to be regarded as a professional craftsman. There are
three grounds for thinking so: she revised and arranged her work
as if for publication, she engaged in private writing competitions
with established poets, and she kept on writing despite her lack of
professional standing in anyone's eyes but her own.

   Todd had to contend with a number of variants which Dickinson left behind in many of her poems. She presented them to the
public as a sign of the poet's amateurism — and of her own
editing skill. Other critics were quick to pick up on the unresolved
amendments as proof of the primitive genius myth. John Crowe
Ransom, who epitomizes the sexist dismissal of Dickinson as 'a
little home-keeping person', wrote that 'while she had a proper
notion of the final destiny of her poems . . . she was not one of
those poets who had advanced to the later stage of operations
where manuscripts are prepared for the printer'.[5] He was kind
enough to alter the poems he printed, 'with all possible forbear-
ance'. To shrug Dickinson off in this way because she was
unfortunate enough not to be published is to blame the victim,
and to accept a crass view of what it takes to qualify as a poet —

namely, sales. One might expect a fellow poet to emphasize the craftsmanlike in Dickinson's work, and revising is a sign of craftsmanship and professionalism. It is Sunday poets who rest content with their first brilliant insights. Dickinson only settled for 'quick' in the line 'Before the quick of day' (1420) after she had considered the possibilities of 'ripe', 'peal', 'drum', 'drums', 'bells', 'bomb', 'burst', 'flags', 'stop', 'tick', 'shouts', 'pink', 'red', and 'blade'. We have seen that she radically revised the second stanza of 'Safe in their Alabaster Chambers', to good effect. Other poems, such as 'Art thou the thing I wanted?', exist in two variants, although the gaps between them are narrower. She went back to poems of the 1860s twenty years later, as the handwriting shows. Among the changes for which she thought it worthwhile to copy the revised poem out fresh were punctuation variations which gave a subtle new meaning — a particularly telling mark of professionalism. One modern critic, David Porter, has alleged that the revision often produces problems of flow for the reader — 'a concentration on line-limited precincts of sound and space at the expense of the larger coherence'.[6] I am not sure I agree with this criticism, but in any case, for my purposes it is praise. It corroborates my point: that Dickinson *did* revise extensively. And revision is a sign of a professional attitude.

So is the ordering of one's work into publishable form, and again, Todd presented Dickinson's work as lacking any such order. It is hardly surprising she was not impressed with the coherence of a body of work which included single lines attached with pins to existing poems, verses on the backs of school programmes, lines in the margins of household bills, one poem written in the rind of paper around a postage stamp, another on a strip of paper twenty-one inches long but less than an inch wide, a poem on the back of a cooking-chocolate wrapper, and a pencil poem written in 1876 on the back of a taffy-pull invitation dated 1850. But Dickinson had also prepared thirty-nine threaded fascicles, containing 811 poems she had revised and ordered into a sequence which it has been claimed Todd and Higginson destroyed. Instead Dickinson's first editors chose poems which 'proved' her religious orthodoxy, presented her as a tragic sufferer, and fell into the frayed and hackneyed poetic categories for which they thought popular taste was ready. She had prepared her poems as a professional, but they were never accepted as a professional's work, and she was no longer there to defend them, or to provide a living contradiction of the myths. The enormous professional success the poems enjoyed after her death was largely based on the personal myths which Todd and Higginson promulgated and which the public snapped up. This is an enormous irony, as need hardly be said.

That Dickinson regarded herself as a poet among poets, even in her isolation, is clear from her brazen habit of jousting with established versifiers in her poems. She often takes a theme from a poem or essay she has read and produces her own completely original version. We have seen this process in 'I taste a liquor never brewed', which teases and teases out Emerson. This is never plagiarism — Dickinson is too deliberately untoward for that — but the sort of exercise which practising writers set themselves. It exemplifies what André Malraux has called the formative process in art — not the imitation of nature, but the imitation of other art.[8] The work of other writers was another source of topics — another explanation of where Dickinson obtained the wherewithal to produce over 300 poems in one year. This poetic tourneying reflects Dickinson's pride as well as her professionalism, of course. It is 'part of an argument which she carried on all her life with published prose or verse. . . . When she reads something that is printed, she pits her skill against that which has won the public stamp of approval'.[9] Duelling with established writers is Dickinson's way of maintaining her honour against the insult of obscurity.

In addition to sending off her poems, revising her lines, ordering her work, and engaging in private competitions with established poets, Dickinson exhibited one unchallengeable sign of being a 'proper' writer: she kept on writing. Anyone who writes professionally has to come up with a reply to the frequent half-disparaging, half-apologetic remark, 'Oh, I used to write, too'. Dickinson never said that: she was prodded, poked at, and patronized, but she went on writing. Of course a chauvinist might call this the equivalent of other women producing antimacassars. But that this *is* a chauvinist remark is clear from the fact that no equivalent slander could be concocted about an unsuccessful male writer: what would be the masculine equivalent of his 'compulsive' production? Had Dickinson stopped writing, a determinedly sexist critic could have lambasted her for feminine fickleness. Dickinson was still writing on her deathbed, in the dark, on scraps of paper. Within her unparalleled enormous output are poems about not writing poems:

> I would not paint – a picture –
> I'd rather be the One
> Its bright impossibility
> To dwell – delicious on –
>
> Nor would I be a Poet –
> It's finer – own the Ear –
> Enamored – impotent – content –
> The License to revere,
>
> A privilege so awful
> What would the Dower be,
> Had I the Art to stun myself
> With Bolts of Melody!   (505, *c.* 1862)

Does the barber who shaves all men shave himself? This poem begins from an equivalent sort of Russell's paradox: Dickinson is writing about not writing. Is the writer who writes about not writing a writer herself? Adrienne Rich says that this is a deliberately ironic piece of false modesty: Dickinson claims to choose the passive feminine role of reader, but *by* writing the poem, she becomes both recipient and creator.

Perhaps, however, the explanation is both simpler and more pathetic: Dickinson has doubts about the enterprise, as most poets do. She was entitled to them, God knows: no one else, except Helen Hunt Jackson in her later years, thought that she was a poet. And when the reviews of her book appeared five years after her death, the same general opinion held. I have tried to demonstrate that Dickinson generally thought of herself as a poet, but that she had her moments of doubt. Now it is time to consider whether anyone else thought of her as a poet, to consider the history of the poems' posthumous publication and critical reception.

After Emily died, Vinnie discovered the packets, or fascicles, in her sister's room. That she knew little of their existence is less strange than it might seem in the Dickinson household, which

114

was a confederation of independent states, as chapter 1 pointed out. When asked later whether she had ever seen any of her sister's poems during her lifetime, Vinnie replied rather indignantly that she would not have expected to intrude on Emily in any such manner. But like Sophia Thoreau — another link between Dickinson and the Concord man given to 'indulgence in fine renouncements' — Vinnie became a great proselytizer for the family genius after Emily's death. It was through the flukey pairing of her Dickinson will and Todd's 'special relationship' that the poems finally appeared.

Todd, with her musical, artistic and literary leanings and connections, could provide the energy and verve which the task of preparing and peddling the poems would require. Vinnie, somewhat of a recluse in her later years, too, could or would not. Whether Vinnie had originally asked Sue to edit the manuscript is unclear. Millicent Todd Bingham, Todd's daughter, claimed that Sue was offered the poems but refused them. Sue contested this claim in an angry letter to Higginson. Bingham is a very partial judge: her fascinating but incomplete account of the publication, *Ancestors' Brocades*, leaves her mother's adultery out of the account, making Sue appear groundlessly vindictive and Vinnie hysterical for wanting to keep Todd's name off the title-page. In any case, Todd undertook the donkey-work of deciphering Dickinson's hand and deciding between variants in the minority of poems for which Dickinson had left no final version. She originally estimated the copying alone would take her two to three years. In the peremptory Dickinson fashion, Vinnie did not offer to help, although she gave Todd sandwiches, lemon cream pudding, and advice over difficult lines — which Todd later claimed was useless.

Higginson was also enlisted for the campaign, although there is every indication that he provided the name and Todd the hard work. Although reasonably enthusiastic, he was also more prone than Todd to bowdlerize Dickinson's writing. Perhaps he was more aware than Todd of what popular taste would accept — or simply older and more cautious. Bingham claims, however, that both editors agreed that 'if Emily was to be read at all, she must be presented in a form not too disturbing to the reader of the nineties, who might be discouraged if a poem did not fit an accustomed mold. . . . So a good many changes were made'.[10]

This is somewhat disingenuous: Higginson did let enough half-rhymes pass to endanger his reputation in the Boston literary world and to shock the English critics, but he also inserted vapid unnecessary titles which often seem to have been concocted for some other poem altogether. Thus a poem about a dead woman is titled 'Troubled about Many Things', and Dickinson's pithy New England speech is often crowned with scraps of hackneyed French.

Todd was hardly a weak character, but she seems to have been caught between Higginson and Vinnie in this enterprise. Urging Todd to be more demanding with Higginson, Vinnie wrote, 'You are acting for me and *not* yourself'. This was all too correct: Vinnie eventually paid for publication — 230 dollars for the first 300 poems, a sizeable fee then — but she never paid Todd. Whether she was meant to became the subject of a bitter wrangle, which exploded after Austin's death in 1895. Todd claimed that Austin had promised her some land as a recompense for the editing work: Sue and Vinnie contested her demand, and won their case in court. By this time Todd had edited three volumes of poems, totalling some 550 verses, and a volume of letters with additional poems. She still had about 660 poems in her possession — those which had neither been published nor included in the fascicles. All this work — a lifetime's for lesser poets — Todd shut up in a camphor-wood chest, refusing to have any more truck with things Dickinson. This store remained hidden for another thirty years.

In the meantime Dickinson's niece Mattie (Martha Dickinson Bianchi, Austin and Sue's daughter) obtained the sole legal right to all the published poetry and sole access to the fascicles, along with the poems which her aunt had given to her mother. This material provided enough poems for three volumes, *The Single Hound* (1914), *Further Poems* (1929) and *Unpublished Poems* (1935). Bianchi made no deliberate alterations in her aunt's work, but she did have difficulty in reading some of the texts, so that her editions cannot be regarded as authoritative. She was also largely responsible for the jilting myth, which Todd had done her best to deny — although she had set up other legends in her populariz-ing lectures. In fairness, this sort of gossip for literati did at least get Dickinson known.

Three years before her death in 1932, Mabel Loomis Todd

opened the chest. *Bolts of Melody* (1945), comprising 668 poems and fragments, was edited by Todd and Bingham (and later Bingham alone) with the sort of fidelity to the text which perhaps Todd would have preferred all along. In any case, it was the nearest to an authoritative edition of the poems yet produced, although the poet had been dead for sixty years. But it took another decade before Thomas H. Johnson produced the definitive variorum edition of 1,775 poems for Harvard University, which had bought the Dickinson literary estate in 1950. Dickinson was unpublished by name during her lifetime, and we have only possessed accurate editions of her poems in the thirty years since the Johnson version in 1955. How has this telescoping of publication affected her critical reputation? And how has that reputation changed?

Dickinson's *Poems* (1890) was published to comments which ranged from the adulatory, in one case, through the damning-with-faint-praise to the vicious. This critical confusion is hardly surprising when the *Poems'* publisher, Thomas Niles, had told Todd:

> It has always seemed to me that it would be unwise to perpetuate Miss Dickinson's poems. They are quite as remarkable for defects as for beauties and are generally devoid of true poetical qualities. If, however, Miss Dickinson [Vinnie] will pay for the plates. . . .

Higginson's prefatory essay, 'An Open Portfolio', intended to introduce readers to Dickinson's work, treated her much as the French impressionists did African art, glorifying her work for its naïve and primitive vitality. He made two patronizing and erroneous assumptions: that she never wanted to publish and that she never revised. Paying her a back-handed compliment on this mistaken basis, he suggested that 'we may often gain by the seclusion of the portfolio, which rests content with a first stroke and does not over-refine and prune away afterwards'.[11] Higginson's essay set the tone for most early comment on Dickinson, which typically bemoaned her lack of grammar and lyrical ability but declared her images ingenious. When she was praised, it was for content, not form. 'When a thought takes one's breath away, who cares to count the syllables?'[12]

We have already seen that editing sometimes worsened Dickinson's allegedly 'poor grammar', as in the case of 'Success is counted sweetest'. But this accusation stuck despite its superficiality. Certainly there are occasions when Dickinson appears to use singular subjects with plural verbs, but sometimes these are subjunctives, of the 'till it depart' variety — with 'may' or 'should' understood. This typically peremptory Dickinson manner is clear in the use of 'be' in the lines 'Menagerie to me/My neighbor be'. Another fruitless grammatical controversy raged over the final couplet of the poem which Higginson titled 'Troubled about Many Things' (187, 'How many times these low feet staggered'), which ends 'Indolent housewife/In Daisies lain'. An English critic sniffed that 'In Daisy's lane' would make about as much sense, and that no poet could be taken seriously who could not distinguish 'laid' from 'lain'. But this is to assume that Dickinson intended the transitive verb here: suppose she meant 'having lain down in daisies'? The real source of these quibbles over Dickinson's grammar appears to be metropolitan snobbery coupled with sexism: Dickinson was seen as a poorly-educated provincial female. This was an ironically ignorant assumption on the part of her English critics, who took it for granted that a New England girl of the period which produced many great educational institutions for women and coeducational secondary schools would have received as scanty an education as an Englishwoman of that time.

Critics were just as troubled by Dickinson's metres and rhyme, or more so. We now regard this attitude towards her scansion with the same incredulity we feel about the eighteenth century's dismissal of Donne as metrically clumsy, but it was the prevailing feeling. Arlo Bates, another of the mighty literary lions who are now remembered largely for their scanty connection with the woman they patronized, wrote in his reader's report:

> There is hardly a line in the entire volume, and certainly not a stanza, which cannot be objected to on the score of technical imperfection. . . . She is not so much disdainful of conventions as she seems to be insensible to them. Her ear had certainly not been susceptible of training to the appreciation of form and melody, or it is inconceivable that she should have written as she did.[13]

118

A year later the enormous popular success of the poems seemed to have altered Bates's opinion: in 1891 he wrote that Dickinson 'gives greater promise of high and enduring power than almost any other American poet of our own generation'.[14]

The only critic to challenge the common scorn for Dickinson's technique was William Dean Howells, who held that the half-rhymes and the pre-Hopkins sprung verse were proofs that she *had* mastered her craft. The critical pendulum has now swung so entirely in this direction that some moderns, such as Porter, criticize Dickinson for keeping *too strictly* to the confines of accepted metres. (One would be happy to see critics damn Dickinson if they could only agree on why: Holland and Ford made contrary complaints to Higginson's criticism about earthiness.) Howells departed from the newly-established convention in refusing to see Dickinson as a meagre imitation of Emerson — he suggested that Heine and Blake were equally likely, but that she was never derivative — and in viewing her as professional rather than primitive.

> Few of the poems in this book are long, but none of the short, quick impulses of intense feeling or poignant thought can be called fragments. They are each a compressed whole, a sharply finished point, and there is evidence, circumstantial or direct, that the author spared no pains in the perfect expression of her ideals. Nothing, for example, could be added that would say more than she has said in four lines:
>
> > Presentiment is that long shadow on the lawn
> > Indicative that suns go down;
> > The notice to the startled grass
> > That darkness is about to pass.
>
> Occasionally the outside of the poem is left so rough, so rude, that the art seems to have faltered. But there is apparent to reflection the fact that the artist meant just this harsh exterior to remain, and that no grace of smoothness could have imparted her intentions as it does.[15]

This atypically glowing review produced, as it were, howls of protest. (To be fair, Howells's argument in the last sentence is dubious because it is unfalsifiable. If Dickinson writes clumsily, it must be because she intended to do so; if she writes smoothly, it is obviously because she intended to do so. There is no way she can be proven a bad writer on this view, and according to Karl Popper's criteria for scientific hypotheses, an unfalsifiable hypothesis is a bad hypothesis.) The *London Daily News* called Howells's delineation of Dickinson's literary pedigree a cover-up for bastardy: 'Now neither Blake, nor Mr. Emerson, nor Heine was an idiot. Miss Dickinson must bear her own poetic sins; she reminds us of no sane nor educated writer.'[16] The poet and man of letters, Thomas Bailey Aldrich, who had succeeded Howells as editor of the *Atlantic Monthly* in 1881, shrugged off the poems' success: 'Miss Dickinson's versicles have a queerness and a quaintness that have stirred a momentary curiosity in emotional bosoms. Oblivion lingers in the immediate neighborhood.'[17] And so it did — for Aldrich's own poetic reputation.

The Scottish reviewer Andrew Lang — self-styled anthropologist and 'editor' of twelve volumes of fairy tales which were actually put together by his wife — was also dismissive of Dickinson's 'formlessness', lack of grammar, and faulty rhymes: 'One might as well seek for an air in the notes of a bird as for articulate and sustained poetry here'.[18] Only 'I never saw a moor' was to his taste though perhaps less to ours:

> I never saw a moor,
> I never saw the sea;
> Yet know I how the heather looks,
> And what a wave must be.
>
> I never spoke with God,
> Nor visited in Heaven;
> Yet certain am I of the spot
> As if the chart were given.[19]

But Lang's review was almost bound to be damning: it began by positing a contest between English and American poetry. Dickinson's grammar could be expected to be poor, he asserted, because that is how 'Democracy' speaks — 'a fault of defective civilisations'. To be fair, he did review another American poet favourably in the same article: one Thomas Bailey Aldrich.

Aldrich was perhaps one-quarter right — half-right is too

generous — in his prediction that Dickinson mania would soon die down. The publication of the third volume of poems in 1896 was touted as the literary event of the season, which could have either comforted or infuriated Mabel Todd, embroiled in her courtroom drama with the remaining Dickinsons. But after Todd locked up the chest and the poems ceased to appear so regularly, less scholarly and popular attention was paid to Dickinson until about 1920 or 1930. The first critic (besides Howells) who presented Dickinson as great rather than merely novel was another poet, Robert Hillyer, professor at Harvard and winner of the Pulitzer Prize in 1933.[20] Even by the time Hillyer wrote in 1922, however, the most patronizing excesses of the early criticism were out of fashion. ' "Quaint", "whimsical", "obscure", "eccentric", these words no longer express an appraisal of her work, and the lazy-minded who once applied them to her have now either given her up altogether or have been piqued by a second reading to closer attention.'[21] Hillyer was ready to substitute 'unique' for these terms, but not yet 'great':

> But was she a great poet? . . . She certainly discovered a magic idiom of her own, which is hers only and can never be imitated. She interpreted New England and Eternity — but both these lands have fallen in favor. . . . I hear much talk about the Greatest American Poet, with Poe and Whitman in the foreground. But there is only one American writer who, I am certain, can never, in any place or in any manner, be subjected to comparison.[22]

The rigid British attitude, too, began to soften around this time. Writing in *The Spectator* in 1923, Martin Armstrong accepted Howells's old comparisons with Blake and praised Dickinson's powers of description, her tranquil humour, and her ability to capture wonder. The acceptance was still diffident, however, and the myth of the recluse unchallenged. 'At her best, she writes poems which are quite perfect. But on the flawless poet, detached from date or personal idiosyncracy, the little New England spinster is perpetually intruding with her charming, narrowly dated, demure yet humourous Quakerishness.'[23] The British public was introduced to Dickinson's work in a new form through Conrad Aiken's edition of *Selected Poems*, published in America and in England by Jonathan Cape, which accepted the standard 1890s view that the poems were formless but nevertheless called them 'perhaps the finest, by a woman, in the English language'.[24] Armstrong was still patronizing towards both women and Americans, but he went so far as to correct Aiken by striking out the 'perhaps'.

Aiken's introduction manifested a leaning which was to become more and more prevalent in Dickinson criticism — the psychoanalytical trend. 'Her extreme self-seclusion' — still the first fact about her to Aiken — 'was both a protest and a display — a kind of vanity masquerading as modesty.'[25] This is fairly low-powered psychoanalysis, no more extreme than much I have indulged in myself, despite my dislike of the extremes in psychological criticism. But by the time the full poetry had been published, post-Freudian updating of the myths was in the ascendant. Ruth Miller has complained that extreme psychological determinism has not taken Dickinson any more seriously than did the editors or critics of the nineteenth century. The poems that she had prepared as a professional were never accepted as such. 'They were received by a world that had assumed the right to decide for itself what it would have from her pen. And the world chose poems that proved Emily Dickinson was a tragic sufferer, a Puritan, a Transcendentalist, a social satirist, a Gnostic, a homosexual, a maiden suffering from an Electra complex, and an Existentialist. . . . One views this second phase of Emily Dickinson's literary history as a rising flood of interpretations that would eventually smash the poems apart, and hurl the fragments against the stolid rocks of critical determinism.'[26] There is now a greater tendency to take the poems as much as possible at face value, but this is not always easy, of course.

No doubt Dickinson would have been highly amused — or insulted — by the academic and literary games which have been played with her poems. Perhaps she would have been less annoyed by the outright insults than by the ambivalent and patronizing praise. She knew her Bible, and was familiar with the fate of the lukewarm. No speculation on her reaction to the history of her own recognition is relevant, of course: she was unrecognized in her own time. I have tried to present this as the inescapable centre to which her poetic existence always returned, in its sad way. Miller believes that Dickinson was banking on posthumous fame: I think this improbable. Poem after poem concerns failure:

My Portion is Defeat – today –
A paler luck than Victory –
Less Paeans – fewer Bells –
The Drums don't follow Me – with Tunes –
Defeat – a somewhat slower – means –
More arduous than Bells – ...   (639, *c.* 1862)

The Service without Hope
Is tenderest, I think –
Bécause 'tis unsustained
By stint – Rewarded Work

Has impetus of Gain –
And impetus of Goal –
There is no Diligence like that
That knows not an Until –   (779, *c.* 1863)

Then there are the many poems about pain, or 'Success is
counted Sweetest' — or perhaps most chilling, 'Art thou the thing
I wanted?' But I have found none of these so moving as the
following poem, which Dickinson wrote shortly before her death.
I would not claim to offer a definitive interpretation of it: all the
same, it moved me because it seemed to be addressed directly to
me, as the 'gentle Reader'. Why not, when this was a common
convention? Perhaps it was not of a lover, but of me — and you —
that Dickinson wrongly thought herself deprived.

So give me back to Death –
The Death I never feared
Except that it deprived of thee –
And now, by Life deprived,
In my own Grave I breathe
And estimate its size –
Its size is all that Hell can guess –
And all that Heaven was –   (1632, *c.* 1884)

Notes

1. Watts, *Poetry of American Women*, p. 67.
2. Mark Twain, *The Adventures of Huckleberry Finn* (New York: Holt Rinehart and Winston, 1961), pp. 122–3.
3. William Winter, 'The Last Scene', *Springfield Republican*, 12 March 1859, in Sewall, *Life*, vol. 2, appendix IV, pp. 742ff.
4. Nancy A. W. Priest, 'Over the River', ibid.
5. John Crowe Ransom, quoted in Adrienne Rich, 'Vesuvius at Home: The Poetry of Emily Dickinson', in Ferlazzo, *Critical Essays*, p. 182.
6. Porter, *Idiom*, p. 97.
7. Miller, *Poetry*, pp. 29ff.
8. André Malraux, *The Voices of Silence*, trans. S. Gilbert (London, 1954).
9. Miller, *Poetry*, p. 221.
10. Bingham, *Ancestors' Brocades*, p. 40.
11. Higginson, 'An Open Portfolio', in C. R. Blake and C. F. Wells (eds.), *The Recognition of Emily Dickinson* (Ann Arbor: Univ. of Mich. Press, 1964), p. 3.
12. Ibid., p. 7.
13. Arlo Bates, 'Miss Dickinson's Poems', ibid., p. 12.
14. Arlo Bates, review in the *Boston Herald*, quoted in Bingham, *Ancestors' Brocades*, fn., p. 53.
15. William Dean Howells, 'The Strange Poems of Emily Dickinson', *Harper's New Monthly Magazine*, January 1891, pp. 318–20, in Blake and Wells, *Recognition*, pp. 22–3.
16. Anonymous review in the *London Daily News*, 2 January 1891, ibid., p. 25.
17. Thomas Bailey Aldrich, '*In Re* Emily Dickinson', *The Atlantic Monthly*, LXIX, January 1892, pp. 143–4, ibid., p. 56.
18. Andrew Lang, review in *Illustrated London News*, 7 March 1891, p. 307, ibid., p. 37.
19. I have reproduced the poem (1052 in the variorum text) as it appeared in the 1890 edition. Dickinson wrote 'Billow be' in the fourth line (not 'wave must be') and 'Checks' rather than 'chart' in the eighth. When I first read this poem at school in the 1960s, it was still the Higginson edition we used.
20. Perhaps one should also include an earlier 'modern view', a letter defending Dickinson's technique which was written by Francis H. Stoddard and printed in *The Critic* in 1892 (Blake and Wells, *Recognition*, p. 52). Stoddard analysed 'I died for Beauty' and found the form a perfect series of parallels.
21. Robert Hillyer, 'Emily Dickinson', *The Freeman*, VI, 18 October 1922, pp. 129–31, in Blake and Wells, *Recognition*, pp. 98–9.
22. Ibid., p. 104.
23. Martin Armstrong, 'The Poetry of Emily Dickinson', *The Spectator*, CXXX, 6 January 1923, 22–3, ibid., p. 107.
24. Conrad Aiken (ed.), *Selected Poems of Emily Dickinson* (London and

New York: Jonathan Cape, 1924, pp. 110ff.

25. Ibid., p. 113.
26. Miller, *Poetry*, p. 29.

Chronology

<table>
<tr><td>1830</td><td>10 December: Emily Elizabeth Dickinson born.</td></tr>
<tr><td>1833</td><td>Grandfather Samuel Fowler Dickinson sells his half of family home (The Homestead) and moves to Cincinnati.
Emily visits aunt Lavinia Norcross ('She is a very good child and but little trouble').</td></tr>
<tr><td>1835</td><td>Father appointed treasurer of Amherst College ('he never . . . lost a dollar').</td></tr>
<tr><td>1840</td><td>Father sells his half of Homestead and moves his family to house on North Pleasant Street.
Emily and Lavinia begin first term at Amherst Academy.</td></tr>
<tr><td>1844, 1846</td><td>Religious revivals in Amherst.</td></tr>
<tr><td>1845–7</td><td>Thoreau at Walden Pond (moves in on Independence Day).</td></tr>
<tr><td>1847</td><td>Emily enters Mount Holyoke Seminary.</td></tr>
<tr><td>1848</td><td>Emily writes to Abiah Root: 'I am now studying Silliman's Chemistry and Cutter's Physiology, in both of which I am much interested.'
Emily Bronte dies ('gigantic Emily Bronte').</td></tr>
<tr><td>1849</td><td>Longfellow publishes Kavanagh (brought home by Austin).</td></tr>
<tr><td>1850</td><td>Ben Newton, Emily's tutor, sends her Emerson's poems.
Religious revival ('I am standing alone in rebellion').
Mother ill.
Father, Vinnie and Susan Gilbert join First Church.
Hawthorne publishes Scarlet Letter.</td></tr>
</table>

1851	Father rings church bells for northern lights. Melville publishes *Moby Dick*.
1852	*Springfield Republican* publishes a valentine by Emily.
1853	Ben Newton dies, aged 32. Emily writes to Austin: 'I've been in the habit *myself* of writing some few things'.
1854	Charlotte Bronte dies. Thoreau publishes *Walden*.
1855	Emily visits Washington and Philadelphia. Father buys back Homestead. Mother's long illness begins. Father nominated for Congress but defeated. Whitman publishes *Leaves of Grass* ('I was told his book was disgraceful').
1856	Austin joins First Church, marries Susan Gilbert.
1857	Emerson lectures in Amherst and stays with Austin and Sue.
1859	Darwin publishes *The Origin of Species* ('We thought Darwin had thrown "The Redeemer" away').
1860	Lincoln elected president.
1861	Civil War begins. *Springfield Republican* prints 'I taste a Liquor never brewed' as 'The May-Wine'. Elizabeth Barrett Browning dies (Emily to Bowles in Europe: 'If you touch her Grave, put on a hand on the Head, for me – her unmentioned Mourner').
1862	*Springfield Republican* prints 'Safe in their Alabaster Chambers'. Higginson publishes 'Letter to a Young Contributor'. Emily writes first letter to Higginson, includes four poems. Thoreau dies (Emily to Sue on holiday some years after: 'Was the sea kind? Kiss him for Thoreau').

1864	*Round Table* (New York newspaper) prints 'Some keep the Sabbath going to Church'.
	Emily spends seven months in Boston for eye treatment.
	Austin drafted, buys substitute for 500 dollars.
	Hawthorne dies.
1865	More eye treatment in Boston.
	Civil War ends.
	Emerson lectures in Amherst again.
1866	*Republican* prints 'A Narrow Fellow in the Grass' (Emily complains of editorial changes: 'It was robbed of me').
1869	Emily refuses Higginson's invitation to visit him in Boston ('I do not cross my father's ground to any house in town').
	General and Mrs George B. McClelland visit Homestead (McClelland was former commander-in-chief of Union army).
1870	Higginson visits Emily in Amherst ('She talked soon and thenceforward continuously — and deferentially — sometimes stopping to ask me to talk instead of her — but readily recommencing').
1871	George Eliot publishes *Middlemarch* ('What do I think of glory – ').
1873	Emily pronounced theologically sound after her father requests his pastor to examine her.
	Austin elected treasurer of Amherst College after father's resignation in previous year.
	Higginson lectures in Amherst and visits Emily (Mary Higginson: 'Oh, why do the insane so cling to you?').
1874	Father dies unexpectedly in Boston.
1875	Mother stricken with paralysis on eve of first anniversary of her husband's death.
1878	Samuel Bowles dies.

Mother breaks hip.
Masque of Poets prints 'Success is Counted Sweetest' anonymously (later attributed to Emerson).

1879	Great fire in Amherst ('only the fourth of July'). George Eliot dies.
1881	Mabel Todd arrives in Amherst.
1882	Charles Wadsworth dies. Emerson dies. Judge Lord seriously ill. Mabel and Austin begin affair (Austin enters one word in diary: 'Rubicon'). Mother dies.
1883	Confrontation between Mabel and Susan. Susan's eight-year-old son Gilbert dies. Austin has attack of malaria. Vinnie ill. Judge Lord has stroke.
1884	Judge Lord dies. Emily has nervous breakdown.
1885	Helen Hunt Jackson dies.
1886	January: Mabel Todd notes in diary, 'Emily Dickinson taken very ill in the afternoon'. Early May: Emily writes last letter (to Norcrosses: 'Little Cousins, Called back. Emily'). 15 May: Emily Dickinson dies of Bright's Disease, a kidney disorder (Austin's diary: 'The day was awful. She ceased to breathe that terrible breathing just before the whistles sounded for six.'). 19 May: Funeral. Higginson reads Emily Bronte's 'Last Lines'.

Further Reading

The definitive edition of Dickinson's poems was published in 1955 and edited by Thomas H. Johnson. This 'variorum' edition — whose numbering I have followed throughout — contains all 1,775 poems. Selections of the poems are also available in paperback and hardbound versions, but the reader should take some of their introductions with a grain of salt, even though their choice of poems and use of the authentic Johnson editions is commendable. This warning applies to the Hughes paperback collection, for example. Editions of the original, mangled Todd–Higginson versions still circulate, and with these the reader should take great care. They can be recognized by the substitution of 'but a Mound' for 'in the Ground' in the poem 'Because I could not stop for Death', and by 'chart' rather than 'Checks' in "I never saw a Moor". Some anthologies of modern poetry still reproduce the Todd–Higginson versions, although usually without the true giveaway to the heavy-handed editing: the insertion of titles where Dickinson used none. Todd and Higgginson also did their best to exorcise Dickinson's famous dashes, an accepted style of punctuation in the mid-nineteenth century but less acceptable by the time the poems were published. If the reader can accustom herself to the frequent dashes, there is little reason to use a Todd–Higginson edition except out of historical interest.

The *Letters of Emily Dickinson*, edited by Johnson and Theodora Ward, are fascinating if only to show how much more clearly Dickinson wrote in her poems. They can be situated more easily in Dickinson's life if read together with Jay Leyda's *Years and Hours of Emily Dickinson* (1960) or Richard Sewall's two-volume biography. Further critical sources on the background to, and publication of, Dickinson's poems will be found in the footnotes to chapters 2 and 6.

Index

131

Printed in the USA
CPSIA information can be obtained
at www.ICGtesting.com
LVHW051054010224
770590LV00002B/191

9 780907 582694